KIDS IN ORANGE

Voices from Juvenile Detention

by Mindy Hardwick

CONTENTS

ISBN 13: 978-0-6928-3068-0
ISBN 10: 0692830685

Copy Editor: Sarah Cloots
Cover Artist: Su Kopil, Earthly Charms
Book Format and Layout: KMD Web Designs

EAGLE BAY PRESS

CREDITS

The following poems appeared in the poetry anthologies published by the Blanche Miller Trust Foundation: "I Am," "I Am From," "Valuable Lesson," "Spider's Web," "Fathers," "If I Could Change My Life," "Remembered" in *Call it Courage, August 2006.* "My Box," "In The Eyes Of My Mother," in *I Am From, November 2007.* "Love For You," "My Name Is Powerless," in *Please Brave Me, November 2009.* "What Seems," "Somehow," "When Darkness Fell on Me," in *Because I Wanted To Be Loved, January 2009.*

Eagle Bay Press
Lake Stevens, Washington

DEDICATION

For the Kids in Orange

DIRECTIONS

POETRY WORKSHOP

Thank you for volunteering to be a facilitator for the poetry workshop. There are a few things you must know:

HOW TO ENTER THE FACILITY

Before you leave your car, slip off all your jewelry and leave it with your purse. You will tuck your purse under a thick, heavy blanket in the back of your car. We have lockers inside the facility, but it's really easier just to hide your valuables in your car. No one will break in. The criminals are all inside.

You will walk up to the double glass doors of the facility. It's a concrete building. On your left, there are windows. You can see pots of flowers sitting on desks. On your right, there are no windows. There are only concrete walls. This is where the criminals live. Along the sidewalk, you might notice the weeds growing in the empty flower beds. You might wonder why the criminals aren't assigned to weeding. We think they are best kept inside. These are dangerous youth.

Dangerous.

HOW TO CLEAR SECURITY

As you enter the facility, you will want to thank the young criminal who holds open the door for you. However, we hope you don't engage for too long. You will notice his jeans sag and his T-shirt is over-sized. You will see his baseball cap pulled sideways over his thick, dark, curly hair. Somewhere, he's got his gang name tattooed, most likely along the inner edges of his arms. You will watch him head toward the probation office while you will wait in the security line.

The security is no different than at the airport, but here you may leave your shoes on. You place your book bag and purse on the long scanner. You remove your belt and hand your car keys to the guard. You will walk quickly through the full-body scanner. If you lean to the left or to the right, there will be a small beep, so please walk straight through the scanner. We don't want to have to use the wand on you. Afterward, pick up your book bag and slip your belt back through your belt loops. Ignore the cluster of parents, lawyers, and families who wait outside the court room and scrutinize you.

SIGNING IN

You will turn right and find yourself in a small waiting room. You will see the pamphlets about gangs, drugs, and violence covering the small tables. Unfortunately, no one seems to read the pamphlets. In a glass cabinet, you'll also see the framed art. There will be colorful pictures of barnyard animals and sunny, cloudless days which illustrate stories for preschool children to read. The criminals created this art. You will want to stop, but you must hurry now. You are only assigned one hour for the poetry workshop. We must keep on schedule.

You will step up to a large glass wall. There is a camera on the wall which will watch everything. At the glass wall, a small metal drawer will open. You will place your driver's license into the drawer. The drawer is pulled inward by a guard on the other side of the wall. In return, you will receive a badge. You will clip the "Professional" badge to the lower left-hand corner of your shirt. You will make sure the cameras can see that you are a "Professional."

Then you will wait until the double doors open. Inside these doors is a long hallway leading to the units. Sometimes your wait will be long when the guards are watching other places and forget to hit the button that opens the doors.

RULES OF WAITING

As you wait, you will feel eyes on your back. You will turn to see a woman who is not much older than you. She is waiting for her son who is to be released that afternoon—most likely at some point during the poetry workshop. She will watch you from her green plastic chair. You will know her wait has been long. She has the look on her face, the one that says she's been here before. It's always the same. We hope you will ignore her. You do not need to talk to the parents. We will do all the communication with parents.

However, you never did follow direction well. You will slip your hand into your bag and pull out a small poetry book with the title *Poems from Youth in Detention.* You will hand her the book. You will know that this is only one more piece of information in a long line of brochures, pamphlets, and booklets which have been pressed into her hands from well-meaning counselors, probation officers, and lawyers. But, instead of glazing over or becoming defensive, she looks up at you and says, "You know my son?"

You know that you don't know who her son is, or even if he's been in the weekly poetry groups. Inside, they are all the same in their orange jumpsuits. But you nod and say, "I do."

Her son is the boy who writes about siblings he has disappointed. He's the boy who writes apology poems to his mom. He's the boy who returns again and again because he just can't get off the drug.

You know him.

This boy.

Her son.

But, before you can tell her anything more, the double door clicks open.

You are ushered inside to the poetry workshop.

THE BIG GANG LEADER WHO DOESN'T WRITE

"Guess she got caught."

"Couldn't stay out there forever."

"There is going to be trouble!"

I lean forward at the hundred-pound table in the girls' unit of the detention center and soak up the anticipated trouble. There is a rush of exhilaration that surges through me. It is familiar and comfortable and I revel in it. In middle school, I enjoyed challenging Dad at the dinner table. His temper flared easily after a few Manhattans, and there was something inside of my preteen self that wouldn't back down.

Dad's and my fights ended up in the green-tiled bathroom with a bar of Dial soap. In the summer, my brother and I found cockroaches tucked in the back corners of the bathroom closet—large black cockroaches that had crawled through open holes in the window screen. Somehow those roaches never emerged during the soap episodes, but they were there every other time we used the bathroom. I held onto the green sink while Dad pushed my mouth to the yellow bar of soap and I panted, with my tongue out, the way the orthodontist's assistant had taught me not to gag on the gooey impressions gel used for my braces. The panting technique worked just as well on bars of soap, and I never threw up. During my parents' first separation, we attended counseling sessions and practiced role-playing with a stuffed, oval-shaped potato with black glass eyes. The counselor told us we could avoid these dinner-time blow-ups. He told us this feeling of anticipated trouble is called "walking on eggshells." It is not a good thing to have this feeling in a family home. None of us ever quite understood this lesson, and years later, I'm really not sure how to live without anticipated trouble.

Each week as I enter the detention center, I feel the same thrill building. Although the guards, locked doors, and constant cameras hanging from every ceiling offer protection, there is still that possibility of knowing that things aren't so safe, and I thrive on that feeling. In all the years of running the poetry workshop, I will never have to break up a fight. When the poetry workshop moves to the school day, I will never have to use the red emergency button in the classroom because I fear for my safety. But fear is always there, taunting me with the possibility of what might happen. Fear lurks along the edges of every poetry workshop, and I revel in that feeling of being right up against the edge of a high cliff, staring down.

I press my stomach against the hundred-pound table as the girls mutter about how when a recently admitted girl finds out that a big gang leader is also booked into this same unit there is going to be trouble. They talk as if a party is about to happen; their voices rise and the guard does very little to silence them.

Which one of the girls is the gang leader? I scan the faces at the table. None of the girls seem too scary to me in their orange T-shirts, plastic sandals, droopy orange pants and thick socks. Without makeup, the girls look to be eleven or twelve, not fifteen and sixteen.

Eventually everyone settles at the table, and I explain that we write poems from the heart about life experiences. There is no glorification of crimes and addictions. I tell the girls they can write about the sex and violence as a part of their experience, but not to glorify, and to watch the profanity. They always laugh when I tell them an occasional *shit* or *damn* doesn't send me over the edge, but I don't want to hear the rest, and neither does anyone else who will read the poems.

I reach into my canvas bag and pull out my poetry books and yellow writing tablet. I place the collection of poetry books on the table.

It's an odd assortment: copies of the detention-center poetry chapbooks written by the teens, poetry books such as *Paint Me Like I Am*, published by WritersCorps, as well as *Things I Have To Tell You: Poems by Teen Girls*, by Betsy Franco. The poetry books and the topic list on my yellow tablet are to encourage writing about the girls' experience and life stories. The detention center poetry program is based on Richard Gold's Pongo Publishing Teen Writing Project in Seattle. Each writer is asked to write from the heart about their life experiences, with the emphasis on empowering the writer's voice so they may better understand and cope with their emotions.

Some of the girls I know from previous weeks in the poetry workshop, but others are new. It's like this each week—a mix of girls who have been in the workshop and girls who are new that week and will need the rules explained. The detention center program director's goal is to run the poetry workshop with kids who are repeat offenders and who have been assigned a stay of at least three or four weeks. But the kids are often switched out of the units on a weekly basis. Sometimes units are combined as numbers drop too low, other times personality conflicts occur and changes must be made.

I've just finished with the rules when the unit door clicks open. A girl saunters in and calls out "One" as she enters. The escort guard nods his head as the unit door closes and locks. The girl carries no blue blanket, which means she is returning from either court or visitation. I'm guessing by the look on her face, and the way she yanks her chair with a hard tug, that it's court.

"I got three extra days." The girl fumes as she plops into her chair. She leans back and two of the legs come off the floor. No one says anything to her.

Immediately, I know this is the big gang leader. The girl holds the power at the table, in the unit, and, it seems, with the guard.

It's her unit.

"Damn judge," she continues. "Three extra days." She slams her chair on the floor, pushes back from the table, and crosses her arms.

The girls all nod in sympathy with her. No one writes.

"Hello," I say. "This is writing workshop. Do you want to write?" I've never been a gang leader, never lived life on the street, but I feel my thirteen-year-old self as it rises to challenge her, just like I once challenged Dad.

"I go by Missy May." She repeats her name to me as if I am slow. "Missy May."

"Fine, Missy May," I say. "We're writing today. Poems."

"I don't write poetry," Missy May says, and smirks at me. "I don't write."

The girls' attention swings to me as if we are in a tennis match.

I take a deep breath. "Try." My voice sounds harsh and cold as my irritation fuels the fire smoldering at the table. I know how she feels. She wants her freedom, just like I wanted mine at fifteen. I know I should act like a grownup. I should use my teaching skills and ignore her until the behavior goes away. But I can't. There is something in her that calls to me. Some primal place that urges me to fight.

Missy May's lips curl into a sneer. "That shampoo over there." Missy May points to the small generic bottles of shampoo on the window ledges. "It makes my hair nappy." She slips her right hand up to her head and pulls on a piece of her hair. "Nappy." Her glare is enough to make a couple of the girls giggle and look down at the table.

I don't look at the bottles of shampoo and Tampax that line the shelves by the doors leading to the showers. I've gotten used to seeing the toiletries sitting out in the open. It's part of the detention center units. "Write about your hair," I tell Missy May.

"I told you," She glares at me. "I don't write."

The table is silent.

It's too much for my patience, and I grip the edges of the table, my knuckles turn white. I am struggling to stop my thirteen-year-old voice, which wants to tell Missy May exactly what I think of her and that nappy hair. I am struggling to stop the part of me that wants to go toe to toe with her and tell her that she is not more powerful than me. I want to tell her she is not my father and that I am the most powerful person in this room.

But, somewhere under that bubbling rage, I am *not* that thirteen-year-old girl, and there is another part of me, too. By the time I am the poetry-workshop facilitator, I have had twenty years of Al-Anon, a few years of counseling, and a lot of experience setting boundaries in my personal and professional life. I have worked with at-risk kids in my classroom and I have loved men who, as teens, might also have been called at-risk. And I have come to learn that I too was once a child at-risk, and my survival skills of being independent, fierce, and powerful mask a scared vulnerability inside. Although boundaries in my growing-up home were more often than not set with shouting and a violence that had me shaking under the covers with my yellow-and-white cat, as an adult I have learned that boundaries can be firm and kind, both when I set them and when someone else sets them with me. I understand boundaries are what makes all of us feel safe and protected, and my job in the poetry workshop is to set this boundary.

The guards tell me I can always send a child back to his or her cell if they are not writing, but I have never done it. Even if a kid does not want to write, I allow them to remain at the table. I know that not writing often can mean the writer doesn't want to face the emotion of the poem. I know this resistance. I face it myself. There are the days when the blank page seems too much and I spend all my writing time checking email and Facebook and blogging. I understand this resistance is a part of the process. I allow this resistance part of the process in the poetry workshop.

But Missy May is not challenging her writing process. She is challenging me. If I don't send Missy May back to her cell, she will run the workshop.

I wave at the guard. "Send her to her cell." My voice is calm and measured. It doesn't give away any of the turmoil I feel about setting this boundary. It doesn't give away any of the fear about how the other girls will respond to this action.

"In your cell," the guard says to Missy May. He stands and his voice is firm.

My heart is in my throat. My palms are wet with sweat. Will she slam back her chair? Throw a temper tantrum? Yell obscenities at me? All of the things I once did to Dad when I was disciplined? Suddenly, trouble feels too scary and too dangerous. I should have thought this through a little more. I could have had a little patience. I could have tried harder. The old tapes play in my head. If I could be something different, things would be different.

Missy May slides back her chair and quietly pushes it under the table. Missy May doesn't say a word to me. She doesn't say a word to the other girls at the table, who are ducking their heads and suddenly have found plenty to write. Missy May walks to her cell. She doesn't look back at us. She doesn't peer out the small window of the cell door. She is gone.

I spend the rest of the workshop questioning if I did the right thing.

I AM

I am a blue diamond spiral.
I am a Cadillac Escalade Infinity and beyond.
I am Skittles from the rainbow.
I am a blue berry tree with emotional pain.
I am a microphone from California.
I am a bed where thugs cry.
I am a pit bull who buzzes around town.

Published in Call It Courage, August 2006.

THOSE LITTLE WINDOWS

The rain sleets sideways across the brick walls of the juvenile detention center. I pull open one of the heavy glass doors and struggle against a gust of wind. Fall in the Pacific Northwest is neither kind nor gentle, but after fifteen years of living in the Seattle area, I have come to love the moody and unpredictable windstorms. I place my canvas bag, filled with poetry books and a yellow tablet of paper, on the security scanner. Removing my belt and dropping it on the scanner, I inhale deeply, as if holding my breath will lift me above the metal detector to a place where I am an observer and not a participant. Today there are no beeps. Airport security is a breeze compared to the highly tuned security system at the detention center.

After picking up all my belongings and slipping my belt through the loops on my jeans, I walk down a small hallway and take a sharp left into another waiting area filled with chairs and tables attached to each other and the floor. Leaflets and pamphlets about recovery centers, homeless shelters, and ways to spot violence cover the small tables. In the three years that I've been coming to the detention center, I've never seen anyone reading these booklets. The only thing read by the waiting visitors are the poetry chapbooks, written by the teens in detention poetry workshop, which I leave on the tables. There are no bylines in the poems. Identifying details of crimes, addictions, and friends and family are removed. There is nothing in the words of the poems to tell a parent or sibling this writer is related to them. But it doesn't matter to the waiting families. The voice of each anonymous writer, captured on the page, is more than enough.

I've walked past the waiting family members with their clenched jaws and eyes hardened with the effort of keeping the sadness, fear, pain, and love bottled up inside. As I pass, I want to tell them I understand this struggle. In the late eighties, I was also a family member in a waiting room of a treatment center, the sterile and cool room empty except for vinyl chairs and tables filled with pamphlets about the family disease of alcoholism on wire racks. Mom thought it would be a good idea if I attended my younger brother's family week at the treatment center. She figured that I, as a senior in high school, could miss a week's worth of classes and not struggle to catch up. Only months before, my parents finally pulled the trigger on their divorce. That final moment of "we are divorced" had been building over a six-year time period.

My sister, eleven years younger than me, was not old enough to attend family week, and years later, I will not remember where she was during that time. When I ask her, she frowns and says, "I don't know. I think I remember a room with coloring books. But maybe I was at a babysitter's or something?" It is an absence I will notice often as I think about those years: my memories are all black and white, nothing is in color, and my sister skates the very far edges of my mind, surfacing only as a distant image as she sits in my parents' dark bedroom watching TV after school. When asked, my brother won't talk much about that time in the treatment center except to say, "I had to have two family weeks. Mom and Dad couldn't even get along long enough to come to family week at the same time. No one else had two family weeks. No one."

Today the detention-center waiting room is empty, and I head for a row of red metal lockers on the wall. Opening a locker on the bottom row, I drop my car keys inside, insert a quarter, and pocket the locker key in my canvas bag. I turn to a glass window behind me and see a guard waiting on the other side. His face is empty and void of expression as he pushes a metal drawer toward me. He says nothing and neither do I. I place my driver's license inside the drawer and push it toward him. He picks up my license and places it on a counter. Without smiling, he drops a plastic "Volunteer" badge into the drawer and shoves it back to me. I open the drawer, pull out the badge and clip it to my jeans' belt loop. Sometimes I receive a "Professional" badge. I want to be a professional and paid for my work. But money for an individual artist who is not a non-profit seems to be a hard thing to find. *book writer*.

Each month, as the adjunct teaching and article writing doesn't quite pay the bills, I advance myself another chunk of money from my home-equity line of credit. It's a loan I opened before I left full-time classroom teaching. I believed I would repay it with that elusive first book sale. In the early 2000s, the West Coast housing market was booming and my credit line was endless. But Dad had taught me well about money management, and I set a limit for myself. If I reached that amount on the loan, I would have to go back to teaching. In the seven years I run the poetry workshop, I will never reach that limit, and I receive numerous offers to increase the loan well beyond what I can ever hope to recover with the sale of the house.

The heavy door beside me clicks open and I step inside a small area of enclosed glass. There is a locked door in front of me and a locked door behind me. I take deep breaths and try to let go. From this point, I am no longer free. Every step I take will be monitored by the tiny cameras on the ceiling. I will have to wait for someone to open each door so I can move into new spaces. Sometimes the wait inside the two doors is long as the guard's cameras scan other areas of the detention centers before returning to my space in between doors. It takes a lot of deep breathing to surrender to someone else's control over my life for the two hours I am in the detention center.

This wait for the doors to open is not so unlike the writing cycle I am in, waiting for my young-adult novel to sell. Young-adult novels are booming, and every writer I know seems a part of that boom. But I am receiving rejections on one of my young-adult novels while trying to rewrite another novel back to my own vision after too many well-meaning critiques during my MFA program. I am selling articles and short stories, but that long-waited for call from a New York publisher eludes me as I struggle to hold to the dream of what my career should look like. It's not that unlike my vision of how my high-school years would be when I dreamed of attending the orange-brick high-school building across the street from our home. I would be a popular member of the pom-pom squad, wearing my red-and-white skirt to school on the days of games. I'd attend fall football games on the arm of a boyfriend who was athletic and popular, and hang out with him in the senior hall. And of course I would be a well-respected member of the award-winning high-school newspaper, following in the footsteps of my parents, who were both journalists. In my hopeful vision, it never occurred to me that those fragile dreams would be engulfed and smothered by trying to keep up the façade of our family secret, which, despite all of my attempts at hiding it, exploded out of every crevice of our two-story home. It takes me years of therapy and twelve-step meetings to understand how my dad's disease of alcoholism tells me in tiny different ways that I am not good enough to have those dreams come true. And that every time one of my long-held dreams moves to fruition, I will fight that same monster whispering in my ear, telling me I do not deserve it.

The second lock on the detention center door clicks open and I step into a fluorescent-lit hallway with colorful green and blue tiles, the same tiles used in the remodel of the middle school where I once taught seventh and eighth grade. A guard escorts me down a long hallway that smells like laundry detergent and food. We pass the laundry room and the stacks of orange T-shirts and pants with elastic waistbands on a shelf. A woman wearing light-green slacks and a matching top walks past us. She pushes a cart with milk cartons and oranges. This is the afternoon snack at the detention center. I peek into the gymnasium: rubber balls and yoga mats are scattered on the floor. It seems a lot better than my own years of high-school gym, where we played endless days of volleyball and I prayed not to be hit in the face with the white ball.

The guard and I reach the end of the hallway. Another guard sits at a command station in the middle of the octagonal pod, talking to two more guards who lean against the counter. There are multiple buttons and cameras around him. As we approach, the seated guard reaches under the counter. The double doors, leading into one of the four end units, click open. I scurry forward into the unit. My heart beats faster, the way it always does in the moment I enter the units. I'm not scared of violence breaking out. It's the kids themselves who intimidate me the most. *Welcome to our unit,* they say as a chair is held out to me. But their eyes see inside to all those secrets I've ever held, and I squirm.

It's two weeks before Halloween and the beginning of the holiday season, and although the stores have been filled with artificial trees and lights, there is nothing in the detention center unit that tells me the holidays are around the corner. A hundred-pound table sits in the middle of the unit and seven chairs surround it. There is a printed chess game on the table. I've never seen anyone play chess, nor have I ever seen pieces for a chess game. A row of cell doors surrounds the room. The faces of the girls peer out of small, rectangular windows. Some make faces at me, others simply stare. None of them look away.

A young lady who I've worked with often in the workshop stands in the center of the unit by a food cart full of milk cartons and oranges. Her orange detention center T-shirt is too big for her and she has rolled up the sleeves. One is longer than the other.

"Do you want one?" Alicia holds out a carton of milk.

I smile at her and shake my head.

Alicia has reached a level five in the unit. She is allowed to be released from her cell in order to serve the other girls their snack. Alicia picks up a pair of green plastic gloves lying on the cart. She slips them on and places one milk carton and one orange next to each place at the table.

As Alicia works, I count out six poetry books and set them next to the oranges. Each year, The Blanche Miller Trust provides the workshop with a grant to publish a select collection of the poetry. After the weekly session, I collect the poems and store them in a manila folder. At the end of each nine-month workshop cycle, I sift through the hundreds of poems to select fifty for the book. I am looking for a cross-section of voices and topics from the workshop. The detention rules say that a release form must be obtained for each poem included in the book. It is these release forms that give us the most problems.

The release forms must be signed by a parent or a guardian, and many times those are not people easy to track down. The program supervisor and her staff make call after call to parents after first trying to find the parents in visitation. Some have gone as far as stopping by the poet's house for a parent signature. But there are always a handful of release forms that are not returned. These poems are not published, and, like a teen returning from court with a sentence rather than a release date, the poems are not freed.

The smell of cleansing chlorine permeates the room, and I chew hard on my spearmint gum. Alicia takes off her plastic gloves and places them on the cart. She pushes the cart to the door of the unit. At some point, a food handler will remove the cart with the trash. I stare at Alicia's long braid hanging down her back: dark hair weaves with blond hair. She's been here long enough for the natural dark to work its way halfway down her back, blending with her blond. I think of my own six-to-seven-week appointments for hair coloring, without which those dark roots take over the center of my part. I've been coloring my hair after stripping my brown hair to a bleached blond with too much Sun-In during high school. I try not to think too much about the skin damage caused by lathered baby oil, which fried me to a deep tan on the concrete pavement of Sugar Creek

Swimming Pool in the hot St. Louis sun.

In late September, Alicia's folder showed two weeks of school days in detention. Halloween is around the corner. Will she be released before Thanksgiving?

"What are we writing?" Alicia pulls out a chair and sits opposite me.

"Open doorways. We're going to write about open doors in our lives." I reach into my bag and take out pictures of doorways. I've taken apart an illustrated book of doors. Each picture shows a different door. Some doors are covered in ivy. Some are wrought iron. Other doors are painted bright turquoise blue.

The doorway writing exercise is usually a favorite. Sometimes I bring white paper and the girls draw doorways. The girls like imagining a door opening before them. They like to talk about the possibilities of what lies beyond that door. Most of the dreams involve a husband, children, and a happy family—things they have never had themselves.

"We wrote that before," Alicia accuses.

"That was months ago." I don't look at Alicia. I have failed her by repeating a writing exercise. But the population at the detention center is always changing. Different faces fill the workshop each week. It's easy to slip in a writing assignment we did a month or two before, and I didn't feel like planning a new writing lesson. I've just gotten another rejection on my novel. This time it's from an editor at a major publishing house. I had high hopes for this submission. The editor requested the manuscript at a conference months before I finished my MFA degree. I told her I wanted to wait to submit the full manuscript until I graduated. She agreed. When I finally submitted the story, the editor held it for a year. I hoped the story was working its way through the acquisition process. But that afternoon, I received a personal rejection. The editor liked the story, but something didn't quite feel right. The voice just wasn't the same as what she remembered in the original critique at the conference.

Alicia opens her manila folder. It's covered in happy Hello Kitty stickers, heart and Christmas-tree stickers. All the stickers are donated to the detention center by a well-meaning church or community group, not really understanding that the teens inside have lost their childhoods years ago, if they even had one at all.

The edges of her folder are bent, and long lines of dates trail down the inside cover. Beside each date is a teacher's initial with the assigned points for the day. The points are for participation in class. Alicia has told me she doesn't like physical education. She receives ones or zeroes for participation. But she enjoys history. They talk current events in history. She always receives full points in history.

I reach inside my bag and hand Alicia a stack of lined paper. The units don't always have lined paper. Most of the time, the only paper is plain white typing paper. The girls like the drawing paper, but Alicia likes the lined paper. Sometimes when I return the following week, she hands me a poem she's written in her neat handwriting.

Today she shuffles the paper into a pile and places it on top of her stack of colorful drawings. Alicia places her hand over her folder. "I just can't," she says. "Not today."

She turns away from me. "It's not you. I just can't. I can't go to that place today."

"Okay." I know the feeling. I'm not sure I can keep writing some days. Some days, like today, when the rejections arrive, I'm sure I will never write another word. I'm sure none of my books will ever be read by anyone. I'm sure I will tuck away this dream to be a published writer into a drawer and never look at it again.

Silence sits between Alicia and me. I will not fill the silence with chatter. I have nothing to tell her today. I have no words of wisdom. I can't reassure either of us that we will both write again. Today the silence is all I can do.

The guard clears her throat and rises from her seat by the door. She shuffles keys in her hands. "I'm going to let the girls out of their cells. It's time for the workshop."

Once the girls are seated, the workshop hour passes quickly as the girls giggle and chat about their open-door writing. Alicia turns away from the other girls and writes her own poem. At the end of the hour, she slides it over to me. "You can keep it," she says. "I don't want to read it."

"Is it okay to include it in our book?" I ask.

Alicia shrugs, as if any decision about her writing is just too much for her today.

The guard motions to the clock on the wall which keeps track of the hour. Our hour is up and it is time for rec. Quickly, I slip Alicia's poem into the folder along with the other girls' poems. I tell the girls goodbye and remind them to keep writing.

Most of the girls call out "Goodbye!" and "Thanks for coming!" But Alicia says nothing to me. Both of us know that she will still be here next week.

I repeat my path back through doors that open and close by someone else's fingers on remote-control buttons. The last door shuts behind me and I take a deep breath. It is only here, at the end of the workshop, that I realize I don't breathe deeply while in the poetry workshop. Instead my breath moves from my chest in a very shallow, uneven rhythm.

I reach the metal lockers and reclaim my keys. Every time my fingers touch my keys, something settles inside of me. It's the same feeling I've had since I was a teen and could finally drive on my own. As long as the car keys are in my hand, I am free to come and go when I want. If I am contained for too long, my stomach tightens and I start to look for the nearest open door.

For years I've awarded a scholarship at the local high school. Every spring, I carry the speech and the award certificate in one hand and my car keys in the other. I always leave my purse in the car. Walking through the doors of the high-school auditorium, I become my high-school self, jiggling my keys and reminding myself I have the freedom to leave and that I am not trapped by the person I used to be.

MY BOX

Inside I have this little box
I surrounded it by a thousand locks
Inside is mine, not yours
If I tell, my tears could turn into sores
I'm scared to even put my thoughts near.
I can handle pain
But truly, it's my number one fear.
I'm sorry okay
I just can't get to the box today
It's not that I don't like you
Or how you care.
But it's so much for my body to share
This is how I'm going to stop
'cause I am slowly forming a tiny tear drop.

I Am From, November 2007

THE FIRST TIME DAD LEAVES

At twelve, I have never seen Dad cry, until he sits on the edge of the bed he and Mom share and tears drip down his cheeks.

"Your mom and I are getting a divorce." Dad's soft voice breaks on the word divorce.

I stare at the shag carpet and wiggle my feet inside my new white Keds. I am required to have these shoes for the Girl Scout pom-pom squad, where I wear a green vest with a large daisy and a green-and-yellow skirt that flares as I walk in our community's fall parade. I am not supposed to wear the white tennis shoes with their little arch support anywhere but in performances, but somehow they have found their way onto my feet today.

"Mindy?" Dad says softly.

"Mmmm…" I say. It's not as if I don't know why Mom and Dad are divorcing. It's not as if I don't understand how my stomach tightens every Saturday night when Dad pours just one more drink. I count how many times the ice hits the glass, and by the time Dad lights the wick on the kerosene lamps that always sit on the formal oak dining-room table that matches the bed in my parents' room, I can hardly eat our weekly spaghetti dinner that Dad cooks using his special recipe. My stomach is too tight as I wait for the moment when the spaghetti sauce and noodles will land on the carpet, dishes will break, and the shouting will begin.

During middle school, I spend hours lying in bed reading young-adult stories of divorce and addiction. I am those characters in the stories, and I am searching for answers I will not talk about with teachers, counselors, or friends. Later this will guide my own career as I write stories of characters dealing with divorce and addictions. It will also guide the book choices I pick for the kids in the poetry workshop, selecting books which detail characters struggling with addictions and abuse.

It's not as if I don't understand this moment I am having with Dad or why the divorce is happening.

I do understand.

But what I don't understand is how this dad who drinks too many Manhattans is also the dad who takes me bike riding on the trails at the university and drinks chocolate milk in the school cafeteria with me. The same dad who takes me to his office, where he spends Saturday afternoon working on his electric typewriter as I work on my homework using pens that hold small soybeans in plastic tops. The same dad who helps me with my Girl Scout cooking badges and we cut up pieces of red and green peppers to place in Saturday-morning omelets. How is this the same dad who knows when I need quiet and alone time, because as a writer he needs it too? How can this dad leave?

Dad tries to explain that Mom and he couldn't work it out. He tells me he tried to attend AA, but it didn't work for him. He tries to explain he just can't make Mom happy. He tells me it's not as if he doesn't love my brother, sister, and me anymore. He says the divorce has nothing to do with us and how he feels about us, the marriage with my mom just didn't work. I squirm on the edge of the bed as Dad's words of divorce hurl me into one of my after-school specials I watch on our color TV upstairs in the playroom with the orange-and-brown shag rug.

Dad's tears run down his face and I look anywhere but at him, focusing on the oak bedside table on Dad's side of the bed. If I open the drawer, will Dad's black bible with the gold zipper be gone? I don't know why Dad has this bible. Dad is not a religious man. On Sundays, while Mom takes my brother, sister, and me to church, Dad reads the paper, smokes his pipe, and drinks Bloody Marys with a stick of celery. Sometimes Dad allows me to skip church and he drives me to the donut shop. We stand in the entryway where the line is three deep. Amidst the pink stools, pink-tiled floor, and pink-painted walls, I order a chocolate-cream-filled donut. Dad orders chocolate Long Johns. We toss in a few sugar-frosted and glazed donuts for my brother and mom. My sister is too young for donuts. Dad calls it The Church of the Old Donut Shop. He tells me church doesn't have to take place in a church. It can be anywhere—even here in a donut shop.

It's something I will remember years later, as I walk on the wide and spacious Northern Oregon Coast beaches, with my dog running off-leash by my side on Sunday mornings. Afterward, I stop at the small tourist town bakery for a gooey pastry, and as I sit on the benches outside the shop and bite into the chocolate, I can almost smell Dad's pipe and hear the rustle of his Sunday paper as he eyes me over his reading glasses: Church of the Old Donut Shop.

When I was five, Dad took a picture of me holding his bible and leaning against a tree in front of our house. In the picture, my eyes cast downward. It's as if I know that one day this bible and Dad will be gone. Dad framed the picture in a round gold circle next to one of my brother in a thick orange coat. My brother hammers at something, an intense look on his face. Mom gets both pictures in the divorce. Every time I spend the night in Mom's guestroom, I will see that same sad girl, framed in the gold circle, clinging to Dad's bible.

Dad tells me he is moving out to a basement apartment. My brother, sister, and I will live with Mom. He will still live in the same suburb as us in St. Louis. He wants to be close to us. They have set a visiting schedule. Every other weekend and some holidays we will see Dad in his apartment.

I look around the room, frantically. Dad's black Samsonite suitcase rests by the door. He takes this suitcase on business trips. Before Dad leaves, Mom has always tucked a worn-out little stuffed bear inside his suitcase; she lays it on top of his clothes. Decades before airport security and baggage checks, Mom has no worry of anyone finding the stuffed animal and labeling it as contraband or terrorist activity. The first time I went to two-week sleepaway camp, I took this same suitcase and found Little Bear with a note from Mom.

When Dad returns from trips, we meet him at the St. Louis airport. We walk down the orange-carpeted hallways of TWA and press our faces to the glass as Dad's plane taxis to a stop. My brother and I jump up and down with excitement as we wonder what hotel room treasure will be waiting for us inside that heavy black Samsonite suitcase. Our favorites are the little soaps Dad takes from the hotel room.

Now the black suitcase sits by the bedroom door, and something inside me tightens so hard I can't breathe.

It doesn't matter how many times I wanted Dad to leave so the fighting and shouting will stop, I hate that when I go to his home-office desk the blue yearly datebook where he records the moments of our lives will be gone. The game of backgammon we play on Saturday night while eating black popcorn will also be gone. From now on, I will visit Dad on weekends and some holidays to play that backgammon game.

From this moment on, our relationship will always be a series of helloes and goodbyes. Every time I say hello to Dad, there will always be a large rock in my stomach, waiting for the moment when I have to say goodbye again.

I bite down on my lip hard. There is nowhere left to look in the room. Dad is crying. And something about Dad crying and this moment is so awful, so terrible, that I will not allow myself to cry. And so at twelve, I establish a pattern I will repeat over the next thirty years. I will tuck away the pain of saying goodbye to Dad in a deep, dark place, and I will never cry.

THOSE LITTLE CHICKENS

Saturday, August 6, 2011
From Dad's Blog: www.asinglemanskitchen.blogspot.com

My children were to be with me the first Christmas Eve after my divorce was final. I asked them what they would like for dinner. "Those little chickens," they all replied. Cornish game hens, actually. For some reason, they liked these chickens. Maybe because the portions were just their size, and they could each have a little chicken on their plate. I have several recipes for preparing these birds, and decided on something simple that could be cooking while we did other things. Bought a small Christmas tree, some lights and decorations, then located several cassette tapes with holiday music.

That evening, I prepped the birds and let them sit for awhile, so the children could see their dinner. When they arrived, the birds went into the oven, and we began decorating the tree. I asked my son to help me string lights. "I don't know how," he said. "I'll show you," I replied. As the lights went up, my daughters played with an electric train set I had assembled. We all put up ornaments and finished decorating with gold and red garlands, then went outside to gaze at the tree sitting by the window. At dinner, they guessed what was inside the little chickens. They concluded it was a lemon in each one (actually, limes). In the background, Christmas carols. After dinner we exchanged gifts and then they left. I felt very good about the evening. It certainly was a more pleasant evening than the previous year, when I was sleeping on an air mattress in a friend's spare bedroom. Sometimes you have to create new traditions as your life changes.

DEL'S CORNISH GAME HENS

1 Cornish game hen per person
3/4 cup melted butter
3/4 cup dry white wine
seasoned salt
pepper
1 lime per hen, quartered

Wash and dry hens. Brush with combination of melted butter, wine. Season cavity with salt and pepper, then season each hen. Place quartered lime in each hen. Bake, uncovered, at 350 degrees, for an hour.

Chuck Hardwick

Divorce, brought kids over for xmas ever they wanted chicken, possibly because it was a size they can fully eat? Had a good time, kids were taken.. This year was better than last years?

WHAT SEEMS

You've seen me as many things
As a groovy chick
Who's fierce and bad.
You've seen me as a bad thing
Sad and lonely
Mean and sketchy
You've seen me in good times
Chill and gravy
Fun and carefree.

But have you seen me
As the real me?

So many defenses to block you out
Because inside I'm really scared.
I love my Mom and sister
I don't want to do these things.
My home's perfect
I should stay there more often.
My heart longs for some stability
And I don't mean a boy
I care too much to go on like this anymore

So, can you see the real me?

Because I Wanted to Be Loved, January 2009.

DETENTION CENTER HALLOWEEN COSTUMES

On Halloween afternoon, I enter the girls' unit and immediately look for Missy May.

I've worried all week. Will she continue to test me? Or will she settle into the workshop? Was there something different I could have done? Did I have to send her to her cell? I've talked to a good friend, Lisa, who works with Richard Gold's Pongo Publishing Teen Writing Project at the King County Juvenile Detention Center. Lisa has been my mentor in writing with kids in detention since I began the work a few years earlier. After graduating with my MFA degree, I attended the Association of Writers Program annual conference and heard a panel of writers talk about running writing programs in prisons. A part of me resonates with the work and finds it much more interesting than trying to teach at a community college, something I don't want to commit to after having just left a high-school teaching job, feeling burnt out. When Lisa and I meet to discuss our own writing, she shares the work she is doing with the Pongo Publishing Teen Writing Project. I am captivated by the honesty and the rawness in the teens' poems. They tell stories that speak to my own story, a story I haven't had the courage to talk about beyond therapy groups, much less write and allow others to read.

The detention center teens' writing reminds me of the National Book Foundation Summer Writing Camp I attended a few years earlier. One of the few adults chosen to attend camp, I participated in a writing workshop with teens from Detroit, New York, and Washington D.C who wrote powerful stories of trauma and loss. When it came time to share my own work, a chapter from my teen-book-in-progress that sounded good to my suburban writers' group, the teens in the workshop tore me to shreds for my lack of emotional honesty. After a ten-year period of not speaking to my Dad, I was about to see him after camp ended, and all of this was too much for me.

My emotions broke and I ended up sobbing while young-adult author Norma Fox Mazer handed me boxes of Kleenex. "Apply to the Vermont College MFA Program," she told me. "I think you'll get a lot out of it." I do get a lot out of my MFA work, but I never forget the rawness and honesty of that first workshop with the teens, and as I read the poems written by the teens in detention, I want to know how to find that courage to write like they do.

Lisa encourages me to seek out a detention center located near my home, and suggests I volunteer to run a poetry workshop. When she tells Richard Gold I am running a workshop at Denney Juvenile Justice Center, he sends up a box of poetry written by the teens from his program. Lisa and I discuss Missy May at one of our bi-weekly writing meetings, and we come to the agreement that sometimes there are no other options, and the most important thing you can do is not punish yourself for someone else's choices.

But on Halloween, my worries over Missy May's reactions are for nothing, because Missy May is not on the unit today. One of the girls mumbles something about an appointment with a lawyer. My stomach relaxes as I hand out lined paper and small stubby pencils without erasers. When I teach in the detention school, we use new, long, sharpened pencils with erasers. But the workshop units are only given the small stubby pencils. The girls' fingers are too long for the pencils and most clutch them in their fists.

Girls have been released over the week and the unit is smaller. Instead of the fourteen we had last week, today there are only seven. By the end of the hour, a few more girls will be gone.

At the end of the table, Courtney bites her nails. She stares at the clock. "Do you think they forgot?"

"I'm sure they didn't," I say. I smile at her. Release: it's always an anxiety-ridden process. I'll often ask the girls to write poetry about a time they were disappointed or a time they had to wait for a parent or sibling or boyfriend who didn't show up. Most of the girls will start the poem, and then the unit phone will ring. A guard will call a name, and she'll be up, out of her chair, a smile on her face, waving to the other girls on the unit and telling them all to be good. And the girl will be gone—for now. Most of the girls cycle in and out of the detention center for low level crimes of drug possession or prostitution. They will return to their lives on the street and the cycle will repeat until they turn eighteen and are booked into county jail.

"It's Halloween." I settle at the heavy table. "I thought it would be fun to write about masks today." I smile and look around the circle. I hope someone meets my eyes and smiles back. It's not necessary to have the girls' approval, but it makes the knot in my stomach ease to know someone likes what I'm doing. The girls wiggle and bump against each other as they peel oranges and open milk cartons. A couple nod at me.

From my bag, I pull out a copy of *The Bottom of Heaven: Artwork and Poetry of the Remann Hall Women's Project.* In 2003, the Tacoma Museum of Glass coordinated a project in which the young ladies at Remann Juvenile Hall in Tacoma worked with artists Darwin Nordin and Judith Roche in an art-and-poetry workshop. As a part of the project, the Tacoma Museum of Glass published a book which combines artwork with poetry. It's something I often share with the units as a way to get us started in writing. I flip to the middle of the book and read a poem entitled "The Face I Show the World." The poem is written by a young lady in detention who shares about the multiple faces she shows the world, from a troubled teen who cries out for attention to an innocent girl who has done nothing wrong.

The girls are quiet as I read. When I finish, I place the book on the table and say, "Where do you wear a mask? Where in your life do you wear a costume?"

The girls erupts in a loud chorus as seven voices say, "We're PUMPKINS!"

I eye the girls in their orange T-shirts, orange pants, thick orange socks, and orange plastic sandals. The plastic soles are always the first thing I hear on the long tiled hallway floor as the teens make their way toward the classrooms in one long line. As the units move between the school day, recreation, and their units, the girls walk with hands behind their backs; orange sandals *click, click,* on the floor. Sometimes when I am in the hallway at the same time as a unit, they are asked to step to the side and lean against the concrete wall so I can walk past them. During those times, at least one girl will always call out, "You coming to our unit for poetry workshop today?"

Alicia yanks on her orange V-neck T-shirt. "Pumpkins. Orange." Her eyes sparkle and she grins at me.

"Pumpkins," I say, and shake my head. "But what about masks?"

"Pumpkins." The girls giggle. They draw long, curly stems on their paper and place the paper on their heads. I look over at the guard, but he looks the other way. Some things are not worth arguing about.

"Masks," I repeat. "Masks you wear in your life. Masks you put on to show everyone else things are fine, you're fine. Life is good."

The girls continue to draw on their paper. None of them look at me. A few write a couple of lines of poetry. I sigh and absently pick up my pen and a piece of paper. Sometimes the best thing is to simply give them space.

I doodle a large box. When my parents divorced, I told everyone

Dad was on a business trip. In my mind, the only people who had divorced parents were those we called "the burnouts." In my suburban St. Louis high school during the mid-1980s, we lived the era of The Breakfast Club. We took those well-defined clique roles very seriously. The "burnouts" wore long, dark-black trench coats, dark eyeliner for the girls, and both genders wore their hair in spikes. It was easy to find these kids because they spent hours smoking cigarettes in the designated smoking area, a small area with benches and trash cans for butts tucked behind the art building. My brother claimed his role as King of the Burnouts with his booming weed business. But I was deathly afraid of being labeled a burnout and would do anything I could to avoid landing in that pool—including lying about my parents' divorce. By the time I graduated from high school, I was better at lying than telling the truth, and it took years of Al-Anon meetings in my twenties for me to begin to find and learn how to tell the truth again.

The girls are still giggling about their orange-pumpkin jokes and I don't mind giving them the necessary space to have their laughter, as joy is often in short supply in the concrete units. Absently, I draw triangle eyes and a nose in the box on my paper. The most talked-about costume in my family is the year I dressed as a pumpkin. We had just moved to St. Louis from Illinois and I hated my new school. I missed my old life, where Mom was my Brownie leader and Dad and I rode bikes on the University of Illinois paved pathways. At my new school, everyone in the fourth-grade class had known each other since kindergarten and I was the odd girl out. On Halloween, Mom handed me one of our many bulky moving boxes. "Why don't you dress as a pumpkin this year?"

I eyed the box. A pumpkin was round. Not square.

"We'll put a little orange paint on the box. Draw black eyes and a mouth. Cut holes for the arms and legs. You can wear the box with an orange shirt and green pants. It'll be great!"

I was pretty sure it wasn't going to be great.

The day of the Halloween party, Dad dropped me off at school with my large box. I couldn't tell Dad I didn't want to be a box pumpkin. He would never understand. Dad loved Halloween and thrived on escorting my brother and I trick-or-treating. Dad's Halloween was full of festivity as the adults treated each other to drinks while my brother and I filled our plastic pumpkin baskets with homemade popcorn balls, Blow Pops, hard candy, and small candy bars. Years later, my brother would take my sister out to trick-or-treat, but by then candy had become something to be unwrapped carefully in fear of razor blades sticking out of the gooey caramel centers, and homemade popcorn balls wrapped in wax paper had disappeared into memory.

The day of our Halloween party, I stumbled into the fourth-grade classroom with my large box out in front of me, and Mrs. Smith frowned and mumbled something about setting the costume in the corner until the party. When it was time to change, all of the girls gathered up their long black witch skirts or pretty princess dresses and headed for the bathroom. I was left behind in the classroom with the boys. I didn't need a bathroom mirror to step into my box costume.

"What's that?" a group of boys jeered as they pointed toward my large orange box.

"My costume," I muttered. I wished I could crawl into the box and disappear. Why did Mom think creativity was such a good thing? I only wanted to be like everyone else and fit in at a school where I was quickly learning I didn't fit because I hadn't lived in our St. Louis suburb since birth. I desperately missed my small Illinois town, where I was one of the popular kids and had loved school and my cozy bedroom where Mom's homemade bedspread lay across my bed and I spent hours reading, drawing, and playing "school" on snowy days.

When the girls came back from the bathroom, as everyone admired each other's costumes, I stepped into the box. No one talked to me about my costume. I moved through the parade in a haze. I just wanted the day to be over. By the time trick-or-treating arrived, I never wanted to see that box again. I told Mom I was making a different costume for trick-or-treat. I slipped into my gymnastics leotard, found a short black skirt and black tights. A friend came over with an extra witch hat to match hers, and off we went to trick-or-treat. I looked just like every other witch we passed on the dark sidewalks, which was exactly what I wanted.

"Did you bring candy for us?" Alicia taps my arm.

I jerk myself away from my memories. "You know I can't bring candy in here," I say.

Alicia shrugs. "You could have snuck it in. No one would have noticed."

Behind us, the guard clears his throat. He frowns at me. It's not good to continue this conversation. I look at the clock: we've got five minutes left. Courtney is still waiting for release, and tears have dropped onto her paper. Quietly, I reach into my bag and pull out a small package of tissues. I hand one to her. I've learned to tuck tissue into my canvas bag. Poetry from the heart often brings tears. The girl doesn't look at me, but she picks up the tissue and clutches it in her hands. "They're not coming," she says.

"They'll be here," I promise her, and as I speak the phone on the guard's desk rings.

He answers and barks out, "Williams. Release!"

Courtney jumps to her feet and quickly moves to the door. She takes nothing with her and does not say goodbye to anyone.

"Would anyone like to read their poems?" I ask. "We have a few minutes left."

The table erupts in a loud chorus, "I'm not done. You can't leave yet!"

"It's time," I say. I am glad to see the girls have finally settled into writing with their small pencils, but the detention center keeps a tight schedule. After I leave, the girls will have an hour of rec. They will be led downstairs to a small, enclosed concrete courtyard with one basketball hoop. Afterward, there is dinner, then free time on the units, and a few of the girls will return to their poems, asking the guard for the small pencils and their folders. But writing time will not last long, maybe fifteen or twenty minutes, before the girls will be shuffled off to their small cells for the night. Halloween trick-or-treating does not come to the detention center.

On the way home from the detention center, I stop by a grocery store and buy ten bags of candy. I live in a new subdivision in a Seattle suburban community which will boom with growth for the next ten years. Our homeowners' association ensures the sidewalks are lined with pink cherry blossom trees, trash bins are put away within twelve hours of pickup, and well-trimmed lawns and two-story family homes seal the package—all of which screams to kids that this is a great street for getting the goods on trick-or-treat night. Kids pour in from everywhere. Cars line our roads for hours, and I've learned to buy the bags of candy on sale at the last minute in order to keep up with the demand.

By five o'clock the first young costumed children stumble up my steps and hold out plastic pumpkins. As the night progresses, the older kids arrive with pillowcases. My favorite Halloween visitors are the high-school kids who come at the very end. They wear only a mask and, speaking through plastic, ask me, "Aren't you Miss Hardwick? The lady who taught at the middle school?" It's never a kid from detention who stops by on Halloween night. *They* call me only by my first name, Mindy, something I insist as I separate my writing-teaching self from the one who used to teach in the classroom.

I tell the teens at my door, yes, I am Ms. Hardwick, and they take off their mask to reveal a shy smile as they remind me of their names and that I taught them in seventh grade.

At the end of the night, I close my door and unwrap the last Snickers bar, which I have saved for myself—Dad's favorite candy. As I bite into the caramel and nuts, I hear the girls' voices from the afternoon workshop, "We don't need costumes. We are pumpkins." And I will remember that I, too, was once a pumpkin inside a box who still struggles with taking off her mask.

I AM FROM

I am from...
    A tweeker shak raided astrew.
    There's nothing I can do.
I am from...
    A closet smoke reeking through
    I can't even move.
I am from...
    A place and color called Blue
    Kicking it with my crew.
I am from...
    A broken and shattered home
    Where jail's always the end.
I am from...
    The corner selling shards where
    Lives always end.
I am from the dark...
    Where evil lurks.
I am from the streets...
    Where people get murked
I am from the other side...
    Where people cry
I turn my face and hide cuz...
    I know that I should have died
I am from this thing called...
    Methamphetamine.

Call It Courage, August 2006.

SPEAKIN' OUR LANGUAGE

"You've got a different unit today." The guard talks to me over his shoulder as we walk past the laundry room, where huge blue scratchy blankets are stacked on a shelf. "It's the boys' unit." The guard is one of the usual escorts, but I can't remember his name. The kids know the guards' names and exactly which shift each guard works and which are their days off, but I've never been good with names and instead try to listen to the kids when they call to the guards for my name cues.

I adjust my canvas bag on my shoulder as we reach the pod of units. The guard points me toward 1E. I step to the door to my left and wait. I'm always a little nervous before I walk onto the units—it's as if I am walking onto a stage. My stomach jumps. It will take until about halfway into the workshop, when the boys are writing, for my nerves to settle, and even then I won't be completely at ease. The nervousness never has to do with a fear for my safety; three guards hover nearby, one on the units and two outside the door. Instead, it has to do with if the boys will accept me. Even after a couple years of coming to the detention center and establishing my presence as the "poetry lady," there is a still a period of time in each workshop when I fear they will see through my masks to the scarred girl who carries her own secrets that she is not writing.

I shift my canvas bag on my shoulder. It's heavy with copies of our latest poetry book, *Because I Wanted To Be Loved,* which I will pass out to the writers.

A unit I have been working with the last few weeks walks by on their way to rec. A couple of the boys nod at me and smile.

"Do you have the new poetry books? The ones with our poems?"

"Yes," I say. "But I'm in a different unit this week."

"I'm getting released tomorrow," a boy says. "I want one of those books." This cry is echoed by three other kids.

The guard who is leading them down the hallway snaps, "No talking." The unit silences and moves away from me, hands behind their backs and soft-soled orange sandals clicking on the linoleum-tiled floor. I make myself a mental reminder to leave poetry books with the parole officers on the second floor of the detention center. I'm never sure if the kids actually remember to pick up the books, but I leave them there just in case.

The Unit IE door clicks open. I enter and the boys are already waiting at the tables. There are only six kids instead of the usual ten to eleven. I recognize only one boy. Alex has a baby face with a large scar on his right arm. It looks like a burn. Did he put it there himself? Or was it put there by someone else?

I have my own scar on my right wrist. It's a small white circle on top of a blue vein. A white line stretches down from the white circle. On a hot, humid St. Louis night, my parents sat on the concrete patio drinking Pabst Blue Ribbon beer from frosted glass mugs. My brother and I fought upstairs in one of our usual matches, which always ended with me screaming down the hallway and slamming my door. We are three years apart and, during thunderstorms, we were best friends. I crept into his room and lay on the floor while the deep, booming thunder moved closer and closer. But during the rest of the time, we were hostile enemies, both trying to survive a war we didn't volunteer to be in.

"Dad!" I hollered from the window. "I am being killed!"

"Go on," Dad called from his perch on the concrete below. "Kill each other off." Furious that no one would rescue me, I placed my hands against the upper window. I pushed the glass and it shattered all around me. Behind me, my brother was silent. I slowly looked down at my hand as blood poured down my wrist. I ran into the green-tiled bathroom and wrapped a washcloth around my hand. It absorbed the blood and, somehow I escaped stitches or a trip to the hospital, but the scar remained years later, reminding me of that moment when I wanted someone to hear me.

I settle at the table with the boys and, after introductions, explain the rules of the workshop. "Write from the heart. Write honest. No sex, violence, glorified language, or gang talk. Watch the profanity." I read a couple poems from our new poetry book and explain how each writer can have a copy to take home thanks to the grant we receive for printing and distribution.

"These poems are too sad." Matt crosses his hands over his chest. "This is my life. I don't want to hear about my life. You got anything else?"

I am good at adjusting to the kids' needs: it's something I learned to do while teaching in an alternative high school for two years. The kids will respond best to me if I listen to where they are for that day. I reach into my bag and grab a book, *Where I'm From*, by Geoge Ella Lyon. I start reading her poem "Where I'm from."

I am from clothespins,
From Clorox and carbon-tetrachloride

"What is that?" Alex asks. "Clorox?"

"A happy home and shit," Josh says. "Mine is like dirt."

"It's a line." I try to explain.

I am met with shoulders shrugging and heads shaking.

The need to please the boys rustles around inside of me. I'll usually fix anything and change anything to fit someone else's idea of who I should be in order to avoid conflict. It's something which I'm wondering if this is a problem in selling my young-adult novel. The most recent rejection tells me the voice isn't as the editor remembered when she read a partial at a conference. There isn't a way to explain to her that the voice changed during my MFA graduate program as four different, well-meaning advisors worked on the story and each had their own idea of how the voice should sound. By the end, I just wanted my degree and was willing to change the character's voice to reflect that goal. It never occurred to me to tell any of my advisors or workshop leaders that I had my own voice for this story. Only years later, after I have sold a handful of books and publishing evolves to have many options, from traditional to self-publishing, do I understand that as a writer, I now have a voice too.

"Let's keep going," I say, and quickly read.

> *I come from a world full of questions,*
> *A world full of food. I am the queen.*
> *I am royalty.*

"She's full of herself. Queen and all," Alex says.

I lose my patience with the boys' discussion. Writing is not easy. I work for hours on one page, only to sit down the next day and rewrite the whole thing. Who are these boys to challenge a published poet? I place the book face-down on the table. "Let's see if you can do better," I say. "Write 'Where I'm coming from.'"

"Write?" The boys moan. It sounds like a chorus as the moans and groans reverberate around the unit. Is the guard going to help me? Sometimes the guards step in and help maintain order. But this guard only shrugs and raises his eyebrows at me. I am on my own, and if he's not worried about the lack of writing, I am not going to worry either.

I hand out lined paper and pencils. I am grateful to my seven years of teaching middle and high school where I discovered if I didn't react to the initial complaints, everyone settled into the assignment. In that classroom, it was easy to distract myself by going to my computer. I spent a lot of time emailing with another teacher friend in a different district. My emails flew anytime I was frustrated, bored, or didn't want to deal with those students. But in the detention center, there is no email. I am stuck in the locked units at the tables, with the boys. I shuffle my papers and books and pretend to be busy. I've never been able to write during poetry workshop with the boys. There is a part of me that can't surrender enough and lose my sense of focus while I am with them.

My lack of attention on them works here too, and ten minutes of focused writing passes before the doors to the unit click open. A new boy is ushered by a guard in the hallway. The boy doesn't look at any of us as he clutches his blue blanket and orange clothing.

"Fresh fish," the boys at the table mutter.

"He's still flopping."

I can't help it. I laugh. I should play it serious, but the giggles start and both the boys and I know I am an easy audience. I've always loved these kinds of boys who can tell the stories, the ones who know how to charm simply by their words.

"Mmm... don't you look good?" Alex says. "You come on over here to me and I'll show you how it works."

The guard in the unit reaches under his desk. A small cell door to the far left clicks open. The new boy walks to his cell and dumps his blue blanket and orange T-shirts onto the bed. I try to get the boys back on track, but it's no use. They are poised at the table, waiting for their prey to come back out.

"Come out to group now," the guard calls.

The new boy shuffles across the linoleum floor. His orange plastic flip-flops click against the floor. He takes a seat at the table and doesn't look at any of us.

"He's in here for truancy," Josh says. "I know it. Aren't you, man?

Truancy?"

The new boy doesn't answer as he crunches low in his seat.

Truancy is not considered a "real charge" by most of the kids who are facing drug, assault, and weapons charges. A truancy charge is often a one-or two-night stay until the necessary paperwork can be filed. At one point there was a separate unit for the truancy kids, but state cutbacks forced that unit closed.

A boy to my left slides me his poem and a drawing.

"He drew you a picture!" Josh hollers. The attention is quickly shifted from the new boy to me. "He drew you a picture!" The whistling and catcalls ring across the unit and bounce off the cream concrete walls.

The guard smiles and doesn't break up the conversation. I roll my eyes and hope my face isn't flushed. One of the downfalls of being with a group of too-mature teenage boys as a single thirty-something female is the flirtation that slips in like a wisp of smoke. It's usually hard to pull the units back to the poetry once we're this far off track, and today I don't even try. I just wait for the conversation to run its course. By this point, my stomach has stopped jumping around and the nerves are gone. I am enjoying the attention as much as the boys are enjoying giving it to me.

But the focus on me doesn't last long and the kids return to picking on the new kid.

"You oughta see the way I hit him at my first meal. Man, it was tight." Josh slaps his fists together.

The new boy pales and moves even further down in his seat.

The boys love to talk about food, and tell a long story about stolen food and claiming property ownership from each other in loud, boisterous fights during mealtime. I know it's not true. Not at this detention center, which is a clean, new facility that seems to be run by respectful guards and staff. But I still find myself caught up in listening to their slang, which is a language they've created, full of its own inflictions and words. Most of the boys come from the Pacific Northwest. The majority of them are white, and yet there is a tone in their words that belongs only to them. Some days I forget to maintain order on purpose so I can try and capture that language as words in my young-adult novels.

The conversation about mealtime antics ratchets up and I listen and wait. It's a part of the poetry workshop that no one taught me, but I instinctively know. So often, instead of going with the lessons and plans I come in with, I have to toss them out the door and go where the kids are in that moment. Sometimes they're restless as too many wait for release or court dates, other times they are moody as they miss girlfriends, family, and life on the outside. And other times, they are filled with stories of life in detention. It's a privilege to sit in the workshop and be a part of their lives, and I know the best way to return that honor is by providing writing that is relevant. The only way to find that moment is to listen.

I absently doodle on my paper as the chatter goes on around me, and suddenly, from listening to the boys, the idea for writing is there. "How about we write about 'the biggest lie I ever told?'"

This time there is no whining. There is a flurry of conversation as the boys start telling their lies to each other.

"Not to each other," I say, and laugh. "Write. Write them down."

There is no hesitation. The boys grab hold of the small pencil stubs and write.

The guard smiles at me, nods, and gives me the thumbs-up.

I take a deep breath and hand out our new poetry books, *Because I Wanted to Be Loved.*

VALUABLE LESSON

I've learned a valuable lesson
when I lost the girl of my dreams.
She picked me up and threw me away,
that's the way it seems.
See she didn't even bother with a second chance
and I don't blame her at all.
But that was the day my heart shattered to pieces
and I couldn't do nothing but watch them fall.
I can't believe I let her slip through my hands
and walk out of my life.
Because who really knows,
she could have been my wife.

So that's the lesson I've learned,
to cherish the things that come your way
because within seconds, minutes, days, months
it just might all go away.
That's what happened to me.
It happened just like magic.
1...2....3....poof it's gone.
And trust me, it was tragic.

Call It Courage, August 2006

BOYS WRITE LOVE POEMS, TOO

"I bet you don't get much poetry from the boys." The guard walks me down the hallway toward the unit.

"They like writing poems," I say.

When I first started the workshop, I, too, believed that girls would write poetry, not the boys. I believed the boys were only writing poetry because they were locked in detention. What other option did they have? They could sit in their cells or they could come out and write poetry. Poetry seemed like a much better option than sitting in a cell and thinking about an upcoming court date.

The doors open and I walk into an empty unit. It's a different unit than the week before, but some of the faces will be the same, as they've been moved around due to personality conflicts or court dates or simply available bed space. The boys are still in their cells and faces peer out small windows. I set out one copy of our poetry book, *Because I Wanted to Be Loved*, at each place at the table. I can't wait to tell the boys we have our own poetry books today instead of the Pongo Publishing Teen Writing Project books. The best part of the grant we received from the Blanche Miller Trust is the kids are allowed to keep the books.

The Miller Trust grant is a special fund in which Blanche Miller, who was a former Snohomish County Juvenile Court Administrator and first woman in the state to be a chief probation officer for a juvenile court, designated a portion of her estate to be used for funding programs that serve court-involved youth. The fund provides grants for artists to work with the teens in detention at Denney and for their work to be displayed in the public. Every year a handful of artists are hired to teach in workshops ranging from glass art to basket weaving. The finished art is on display in a glass case on the second floor of the court building, outside the probation office. The poetry books are distributed in the waiting room at the detention center as well as handed to guards, lawyers, court officials, and educators. I also drop copies of the books at our public library, which are set in display racks outside the library to be taken and kept by teens or adults who might share them with teens. And I do a large mailing to interested parties in other parts of the country who also work and write with teens in juvenile detention.

Once I've settled myself at the table, the guard walks to each small cell and unlocks the door with a set of keys.

"Those ain't the books we've had," Josh says as he steps up to the table and sits down. His eyes droop and I wonder if his sentencing date is coming up and he's not sleeping.

I pick up one of the yellow paperback books. "These are our books. Poems written by Denney kids."

"Where's the staples?" Nathan snaps the rubber band tied around the book. It holds the pages together at the spine. Before I bring the books to detention, I spend twenty minutes removing all staples and replacing those staples with rubber bands.

"No staples," I say. "It's a rule of the detention center. Any pamphlet or booklet has to have all staples removed." Apparently, at one time kids took out staples from a twelve-step booklet and used the staples to cut themselves.

A couple boys snap the rubber bands. One boy pulls off the rubber band and wraps it around his wrist. I wonder if rubber bands are any safer than staples.

"Can we keep these?"

"Yes," I say. "These books are yours to keep."

"Is mine in here?"

I looked up into Jesse's dark eyes. He's been with me a lot in the poetry workshop, and I selected a couple of his poems. But we didn't receive a signed parent or guardian release form back.

"Jesse," I say slowly. I'm not quite sure how he will handle the news. I never know what will set a kid off. What small thing will trigger a sea of anger? It's always there—just simmering under the surface. Someone arrives back from a visitation that doesn't go well or a lawyer doesn't provide the hoped-for response about an upcoming court date. The worst irritations are the ones that bubble up from within the units themselves. Kids are clustered together for days at a time, eating, living, and going to school together, and this can set off tempers which are already on the hot side. One wrong look or word from someone and tempers flare. It reminds me of those childhood dinner tables where meals could easily turn into yelling matches between my parents and escalate into thrown dishes and shoving matches. Dinner is still not an easy meal for me, especially on Saturday night, when I can still hear the tunes of Fleetwood Mac, smell the simmering spaghetti sauce, and hear the ice in Dad's glass as he fills it from the liquor bottles kept inside the dining-room sideboard.

"We did pick a couple of your poems. But, "I pause "there was no release form."

Jesse shrugs as if the news isn't really news to him. "That's okay. I bet I know some of the other people in here." He thumbs through the book while I feel sadness for him. Things don't work out his way and it's something he expects rather than being an exception. It's no different than how I am beginning to feel when I see my self-addressed stamped envelope back in my mailbox from another agent or editor. It's something I am expecting, rather than receiving an acceptance.

"Why are there no names on these poems?" Josh waves his book around in the air pages rippling like a flag.

"Rules of the detention center," I say. "The writers have to be anonymous."

"But those other poetry books had names," Josh points out.

I shake my head and smile. Perceptive and direct is how I describe the kids in detention, two qualities my brother also has, and it never ceases to amaze me at how he can get to the bottom of whatever situation is facing him with a little tenacity. It's a trait that serves him well as he moves through his life driving a buggy in the French Quarter of New Orleans and later, running his own tour company in Buenos Aires, and then to a job as a day-trader.

"Yeah," Jesse jumps on the bandwagon. "How come the other book had names on their poems?"

"The Pongo Publishing Teen Writing Project is different than our workshop," I explain. "The kids didn't use their real names. They made up names and only used first names with last initials."

"You got any love poems in here?" Jesse asks, the issue of names over and something else biting at the boys' heels.

"Yeah." There is a chorus of voices. "I want to read some love poems."

"Actually," I say, "there are two love poems in the book."

"Where?" There is a mad scramble as the boys thumb through the books, hunting for the love poems.

Quickly, I flip toward the back. As the editor of the book, I know the poems well. After we get the release forms, I spend a couple days typing poems. I work my way around handwriting I can't always read, and sometimes guess at a writer's word choice. I quickly discovered that when the boys read the poems in workshop, they often insert a word or two that aren't included in the poem. The other thing I discovered is that a teen's own voice will carry the poem better as he or she reads it aloud in workshop than when I go back and read the printed words. When I type the poems,

I stay true to each kid's voice and don't insert words or change lines. The poems belong to the kids and I make sure they're printed in the book as the kid wrote them. My own experience with being edited on short stories and articles is mostly positive, and I enjoy going through editors' notes, making corrections and notes about where my common errors occur. But occasionally there will be a story or article which comes back to me so badly filled with word changes and line edits, it will take all I have to grit my teeth and move quickly through the manuscript, accepting the changes and then returning the writing back to the editor with a cheery email thanking them.

"Before I read these to you," I say, "I want to tell you a story about these two poems."

The boys look up at me. Even the guard in the unit is watching me.

"When we sent the release form to this young man and asked him if we could include his poem, he sent another poem back with his signed release form. He asked that we not only include the first poem, but we also include the second."

I read the first poem to the boys as they follow along in their yellow books. The poem is about a boy who loves a girl and how he wants her to be his bride. He's expressing his love to her and hoping she'll wait for him to get out.

"That's pretty good," Jesse says.

"That's just how it was with me," a boy says. His voice is filled with emotion. "My girl, she was all crying and shit."

The boys at the table shake their heads. The stories start pouring out. Each boy has a story of a girl who they either left on the outs, who is having their baby, or who they're going to be with forever when they get out.

I let them talk for a minute or two, then say, "So you want to hear the second poem?"

The table suddenly gets real quiet.

I read the second poem, which is about losing the same girl. The boy loses her because he is serving a long-term sentence and can't stay with her during that time.

When I am finished, not one boy says a word at the table. Instead, they look down, they look at the floor, and they pick at their cuticles.

Finally Jesse says, "Man, she better wait for me. I'm going to kick some you-know-what if she don't."

And suddenly the room explodes with tales of who they're going after when they get out if the girl doesn't wait.

The guard shakes his head at me and frowns. I've got to get the workshop under control.

But before I can say anything Nathan asks, "Are we going to write love poems?"

"Love poems?" I ask.

"Yeah," Nathan says. "I got a lot to say."

"Hand me that paper," Jesse says.

Suddenly, the boys are passing out paper, grabbing two and three sheets, and beginning to write. I look around the table and I am startled by the intensity. They lean over their paper and grip pencils as if I'm giving them the test of their lives. At the unit desk, the guard returns to staring at his computer. "Where's the rhyming dictionary?" Jesse pops his head up and looks around the table.

Quickly, I dig into my bag for the dictionary. It's a simple rhyming dictionary that I've had since I taught seventh graders. My last name is still written in large black letters on the top spine. I don't think it was ever a hot item with my seventh graders. But the rhyming dictionary is a big hit with these teens. I bring the book to every workshop, and the pages are bent and creased.

I place the book on the table as Josh and a couple other boys copy poems from some of the Pongo Publishing Teen Writing Project books, as well as the Denney books.

"What are you doing?" I whisper as I tap their papers.

Josh turns a deep red. "I couldn't come up with the words of what I wanted to say to my girl, so I thought I'd copy these poems."

"That's stealing!" Jesse yells from the other end of the table. "You stealing poetry."

"Is it stealing?" Josh asks.

"Well," I say. "Are you going to say that you wrote it?"

"No," Josh shakes his head. "No. I'll be real honest and say that someone else wrote it. I just want her to have a poem."

"I once got my girl this great card," Nathan says from the left side of the table. "She was all crying over the card. Girls love this shit."

"My girl is going to be crying when she reads this poem." Jesse leans back in his chair. He slaps his hands together, then bends over and continues to press hard with his pencil and write. Suddenly he looks up at me. "Give me a piece of paper," he says. "I want to write my own poem. I know what I want to say now."

I smile and hand him a new sheet of paper and wonder if any of the boys I once loved thought about writing me poems, and what they might have said.

IN THE EYES OF MY MOTHER

In the eyes of my Mother,
I am a failure.
I am a juvenile punk

In the eyes of my Mother
I am a low-life punk.
I am not the son she knew.

I want to change

In the eyes of my Mother

I Am From, November 2007.

A TIME I TOLD A LIE

The next week I am early to poetry workshop and sail through the metal detector. Before arriving at the detention center, I've picked up my mail and opened one of my returned self-addressed stamped envelopes. There is a request for a full manuscript from a mid-sized publisher. A couple hours later, my feet still don't touch the ground as I whisk around the corner and into the lobby. I drop my keys into the locker and wait behind a man dressed in jeans and a dress coat. I hear him tell the guard that he is clergy and will meet with the kids. The guard motions for him to step to the side where another guard will escort him into the visiting room. I slip my license into the drawer as the minister says, "But she gets to go into the units, why can't we?" It's something I'm never sure how to answer and I don't get to hear the guard's response. Why am I allowed onto the units and the ministers meet with the kids in the general waiting room? Is it just the scheduling or is it something more? Something I don't see?

Once I am through the locked doors, a guard walks me down the hall to the lower floor pod. It doesn't take long before 2W clicks open and I enter the girls' unit. The unit floor is empty and small faces peer at me from the square cell-door windows that line the unit. A cart filled with milk cartons and oranges sits to the side of the table. The poetry workshop takes place thirty minutes after the guards change shift. During the thirty minutes between school and poetry workshop, the teens are locked into their small cells with books for silent reading. They have another silent reading period in the morning when the guards take their mandatory break. The teens in detention devour young-adult books like the latest street drug, and when

I move the workshop to the school day, the school program director and I will write grants for buying young-adult novels to be added into the poetry workshop curriculum.

The guard hands me a stack of paper and the small pencils stubs. I open my bag and lift out a yellow tablet and a handful of poetry books. I've scrawled ideas for today's workshop on the yellow tablet, reminding me of my dad's Saturday morning chore list for my brother and me, which he wrote on his yellow tablet and plastered to the refrigerator. Even when I am an adult and visit Dad, he still uses his yellow tablet of paper to write down things he wants to do with me during the visit.

The guard clears his throat and I look up to see the unit's roster in his hand. I smile and take it from him. Glancing down at the page, I see *Melissa Jackson* on the roster. My heart leaps and my good mood sizzles. It's been three weeks since I last saw Missy May. Will she still be angry?

One by one, the guard opens seven different cell doors. The girls stream into the room. Their plastic sandal shoes slap on the floor. There is a flurry of voices as the girls settle themselves at the table.

"Are these the new poetry books? Can I have one?"

"What are we writing today?"

The guard hands out the snack and girls open up milk cartons and peel oranges.

Missy May slips into the chair across from me. Her brown frizzy hair flies everywhere. The girls are required to wear rubber-bands in their hair— the same kind of rubber-bands I use to keep my manuscript pages together. But Missy May has escaped the rubber-band rule for now.

"Melissa," I read from the roster.

"My name is Missy May. Not Melissa."

"The roster says your name is Melissa." I stare down Missy May in my best teenage bad-girl-self stare.

"The roster is wrong." Missy May's eyes sparkle. She leans forward in her seat and places her thin arms on the table. "It's wrong."

"Fine," I say, not willing to make a big argument over her name. "Missy May." I continue down the roster calling names. No one else corrects me about their name. When I finish, I place the roster to the side.

"I got in some trouble last time," Missy May blurts. Missy May's lack of impulse control is something I will see over and over during the years she cycles in and out of the detention center. The guards say it's what causes her trouble on the outs. I suspect it has more to do with her temper.

"Yes," I say. "You did. But it's not going to happen this week, right?"

"I don't know." Missy May shrugs her shoulders and looks away from me. "It could."

"Have you ever gotten in trouble?" Alicia asks me. Her voice is quiet and her long strawberry-blond hair is pulled back by a rubber band. I imagine her at night as she pulls out the rubber bands; her hair catches against the rubber and pulls and tears at her scalp. No one hears her cry as she tosses the rubber band to the floor and tucks herself under the scratchy blue blanket. She rolls over on her side, knowing there will not be a comfortable spot on the thin mattress tossed over the wood board in the small cell with the concrete walls.

Alicia's light-blue eyes meet mine. After months in detention, the cloudy haze of street drugs has lifted from her eyes and her complexion is clear. Alicia's sentence at Denny Juvenile Justice Center is rare. Most kids do not stay longer than three or four weeks, and after sentencing are moved to long-term state facilities to serve time which can be months to years. I'm not sure why Alicia's time is so long and I know I'm not supposed to ask.

I slowly look around the circle and seven girls meet my eyes. A couple of the new girls wear blank looks. Their eyes are clouded by recent intakes, upcoming court dates, lawyer visits, and drug use from the outside. Two girls who have been in detention for a week cross their arms over orange V-neck T-shirts. One girl's arm has tracks along the inside, her skin carved into long, jagged lines.

"Did I get in trouble?" I repeat the question. The girls aren't asking me if I got in trouble. The real question is, "Can you relate to us? Or are you one of them?" Them. The counselors, teachers, and clergy who come pass out packets, without staples: packets about self-esteem, bible readings, and checklists for healthy living. The ones who are not allowed onto the units, where I am.

I am not one of *them.* But how do I explain?

I am a master at hiding what I don't want to reveal. I'm never sure how to explain the feeling of why it's easier to lie than to tell the truth. It's something so engrained in me, like an invisible DNA, that I can't even form words around the facts. In therapy I am told it has to do with not wanting to be found out, a shame of what people will think if they know the truth. But even this does not really explain why years later, as an adult, I can still not form the words around the truth. My brother, with his own years of therapy and twelve-step groups, claims it's more like a post-traumatic stress disorder that we both have, something I consider. There is a walled-off separation in both of us, although each of us presents a confident face to the world, there is a part of us we don't trust to reveal to others.

During the poetry workshop, I shuffle papers and thumb through poetry books looking for the perfect poem. I am busy. Very busy. Sometimes a teen will lean over and quietly whisper, "Why don't you write?"

"Oh." I wave my hand airily. "I want to be able to hear your poems!" I smile brightly. It's a smile which masks anything I don't want to talk about. I am an expert at smiling, and everywhere in my life, it works. And if I can't smile and feel the emotions crashing too hard against me, I retreat inward, pulling myself into my home, and lying in my bed for hours as the emotions rage in a storm of their own. But the teens in juvenile detention know all about that smile. They're masters at it themselves, and so here I have a small pit in my stomach that tells me they can see right through that smile and know I am hiding something.

"Did you get in trouble?" Alicia repeats the question.

"Yes," I say slowly. I have been with the girls enough to know they respond best to those who are like them.

Seven girls stare at me. Even Missy May is focused on me. Her eyebrows lift upward as if she is waiting, waiting to hear if I'm really going to tell a great story about a time I got in trouble. I look around the table and meet each girl's eyes. It's the one thing I insist for the workshop. The tables need to be arranged so we can each see each other, and I always sit with the girls in the circle. It's something I learned in my early years of teaching middle-school language arts. "Be sure to sit with your students in the sharing circle," my education instructors drilled. "It makes you seem more approachable." But the educators didn't tell me about the scary moment of telling the truth to a circle of girls wearing orange.

"What did you do?" Alicia asks. The room seems to hold its breath like an underwater swimmer who is trying to see how far she can be pushed before needing to come up for air.

"I used to steal my mom's credit card." I don't look away from the girls when I speak. I stare directly at them.

There is no collective gasp. There is no jeering or judging. Instead there is a quiet, calm waiting.

I tell the girls how I attended a large St. Louis suburban high school. It was important to wear the latest fashion in order to be seen as one of the cool people. Years later, when my sister shuffled off to high school in her hooded sweatshirts and baggy jeans, I only shook my head. In 1986, we never would have dreamed of showing up to school in soft, baggy flannel pants or hooded sweatshirts. I'm not even sure we would have slept in them. Instead, we owned multiple pairs of red, blue, black and white dress-shoe flats, enough shoes to match our short skirts. We carried Gucci purses and gold bangle bracelets and earrings dangled from our wrists and ears.

I've never dressed as expensively or as well as I did during high school.

The most important clothing was skin-tight Jordache jeans. The jeans cost more than months and months of my babysitting jobs, and Mom didn't have money to spend on Jordache jeans. But I believed Mom's credit card offered unlimited possibilities. Didn't she charge my back-to-school clothes on that same credit card? If I made up a few little lies, she'd never know the difference.

I slipped the brown credit card with the white lettering, *Famous Barr,* out of Mom's purse and into my own and headed to the mall. Then I charged just one pair of those fabulous, skin-tight Jordache jeans. I clutched the bag to my chest, and as Mom pulled up to the curb, I told her it was a shirt I bought with babysitting money. A few days later, I slipped on those fabulous, skin-tight jeans and headed across the street to the high school. My rationale was since I looked just like everyone else, everyone would think my life must be fine like everyone else's. It didn't occur to me that our family life crept out of the seams of our two-story, orange-painted house across the street from the high school. The house was never supposed to be orange, but in a strange mix of color at the paint shop the color blended wrong, making the home stand out among the other two-story brick and sedately painted houses which lined the curved road across from the senior parking lot of the high school.

When Mom's credit card bill arrived, my future in young-adult storytelling started. "Maybe someone else is using your card," I told Mom. "Maybe you should call. You know, fight the bill?"

Mom sat at the scratched yellow kitchen table. She smoked a Salem menthol cigarette from the green pack that she kept at the top of the kitchen cabinet with our Hostess Ding Dongs and Twinkies. When Dad lived at home, he was always stealing Mom's cigarettes and trying to get her to stop smoking. No one mentioned Dad's pipe. By the time my brother and I were in high school, both of us picked up smoking too. I took advantage of senior-year open lunch and walked across the street with a friend, where we smoked our lunch from my bedroom window and gossiped about who was leaving and coming with who in the parking lot. My sister found me one afternoon. I had gotten lax about covering my habit with breath mints and huge spurts of Jean Naté. She told Mom, and although I received a shake of the head, Mom was too engulfed in a full-time job, a house too big for her to manage, and dating a man she'd met in the twelve-step programs who called her every morning at six a.m. She said nothing about my smoking. The same was true on the day the credit-card bill arrived. Mom didn't question me, and I realized how easy it was to lie and manipulate in our splintered family.

But the jeans are not just a one-time story, and like an addict who needs a fix, when they shrank in the wash, I needed another pair of jeans. I slipped the card out of Mom's purse, and I charged just one more pair of those fabulous jeans.

When the next bill arrived, again I denied everything. But the lie cracked like a sidewalk erupting from tree roots, something I wouldn't realize until years later, when I received my own Nordstrom credit card statement and read the detailed charges for every purchase I had made. Mom had always known I was using her card.

At the end of my story, I look around the table. A couple girls nod their head. A couple mutter, "Man, you oughta been caught."

"You're just like us." Missy May's voice is clear and strong. "You stole. But..." she stares at me. "Your mom didn't press charges."

"Yes," I say. "You are right." There's another story from about that same time period which I don't tell the girls. It's not because I don't want to tell them, but because the story is so deeply buried inside me that I'm not sure I can form the words to tell it. It's an image that comes to me, rather than words. An image of shame and embarrassment at being found out. Dad had just moved out of the house and, unable to cope with my emotions, I was taking it all out on Mom with attitude and name calling. Mom called a family friend who was a police officer to talk to me. The police officer threatened me with juvenile detention if I didn't get my act together and respect Mom. I burst into tears, petrified of the threat and unable to tell the officer that all I wanted was my dad.

"Can we write about lies?" Alicia asks. "I've got a good story to tell."

"That would be a great idea," I say. "How about you write about a lie you told?" The prompt is the same one I gave the boys' group a few weeks ago, but this one comes out of a different place. It's not bravado and charm, instead it's honest and real, built out of my own story about lies.

Six heads bend over lined notebook paper, and the scratching of pencils on paper fills the room. I make notes on my paper about a character I am working on in my young-adult novel. She's not quite coming together. In the story, my character is too perfect. But now I think about my own experience. Is it possible to give my character a bit of my own experience with lying? I jot down ideas in a long list on my yellow tablet. When I am done, I sense someone watching me. I look up at Missy May. She twirls a pencil between her fingers and nods to me. Her paper is blank.

I let her be.

Lies do not turn into truth easily.

SPIDER'S WEB

The spider web inside me gets tangled.
When I use drugs, I get stuck.
When I use drugs, I fly right into the web.
Caught, stuck, and struggling to get out.

Call it Courage, August 2006.

WHEN WE MEET ON THE STREET

On a sunny spring day, two teen boys walk toward me in a half-strut, half-swagger across the Lowe's parking lot. The boys' arms swing at their sides as if they are airplane propellers. Their voices reach me first. "We ran out of gas. We've got this big boat of a car. It's parked on the hillside two blocks away. His girlfriend is inside interviewing for a job. He has to get to drug court."

The boys are thin and have narrow faces. Their hair is greasy and sticks to their heads. They wear baggy jeans which hang at their hips, T-shirts, and oversized tennis shoes. By this point, most people would be in their car, if not headed to find an employee of Lowe's. But I wait. I'm pretty sure I know these boys from detention center poetry workshop.

"Do you have some cash?"

"I have two dollars," I say.

"Can you get some?" One of the boy smiles at me in that look I know all too well from the workshop. "Please, poetry lady," he says.

"My ATM is pretty far away." It's not that I can't drive to the nearest ATM. The problem is whether I believe them. After living with my brother's booming weed business during high school, I am all too aware how cash can be easily spent on other things, like cigarettes or a trip through Taco Bell after a night partying. I am also aware of how easy it is to lie after I found my beloved bike in pieces on our garage floor. My brother told me he and his friend just wanted to see how it worked. They promised to reassemble the bike, but the parts were sold off for cash and the bike lay in pieces on the floor until it was finally hauled away in the trash when I went to college. I didn't get another bike for over a decade, and when I did, I also bought a large, heavy-duty lock which threads through the tires and I keep on the bike at all times I am not riding it.

When we reach the door, Ryan grabs a cart, and the boy whose name I can't remember struts by my side. The doors glide open and Ryan rides the cart through Lowe's. I have a hard time trying not to laugh, and at the same time, not tell him to stop.

Ryan rides the cart like a skateboard. He dodges people and aisles. I worry someone will stop us and kick us out of Lowe's, but no one seems too concerned. Maybe it's the sunny spring day, or maybe it's just that people are too busy caught up in the worries of a failing housing market to worry about a teen cart-boarding down the aisle at Lowe's.

I walk behind Ryan and his wild cart ride. The other boy walks beside me. "I'm sorry," I say. "Can you remind me your name?"

"Drew. My girl is interviewing for a job."

"That's great," I say, "Do I know her?"

"Nah. She's not a detention girl."

The girls in detention *ooh* and *ah* over the boys, but unless the boy came in with the girl already as his girlfriend, most of the boys don't pay attention to them. It makes me sad for the girls, who spend a lot of time trying to watch the boys through the heavy windows of the pod units. But Drew verifies for me what I've suspected. The boys in detention aren't paying attention to the girls who wear orange jumpsuits like them.

As we follow Ryan, a young lady wearing jeans and a colorful sweater steps up beside Drew. Her lips are decorated with just a hint of pink and she has a small dab of mascara on her eyelashes. I smile at her. She shyly smiles back at me and slips her hand into Drew's.

"Hey," Drew says. "How'd the interview go?"

I pick up my pace to give Drew and his girl some space. I know this girl better than she thinks. I was once her, twenty and tucked under the arm of my sober boy, believing in my own happily-ever-after.

I turn to holler at Ryan. "Down here. Furnace filters!"

Ryan abruptly U-turns the cart. He rides to where I am standing and screeches to a halt inches from my feet. I'm glad to be wearing shoes that cover my toes.

"What kind of filter?" Ryan asks.

I look down at my list and rattle off the measurements.

Ryan scans the boxes of filters before he says, "Here you go." He yanks hard on a filter placed in the middle of a stack. Cardboard boxes fly everywhere. Filters drop onto the floor and scatter.

"Maybe not that one." I check the measurements on my list. We are just a couple inches off. "I think it's this one." I grab a filter on a top shelf and pull. Three filters fly off the shelf and land on the floor. Changing the furnace air filter is turning out to be harder than I thought.

Ryan kneels on the floor and grabs a handful of filters. He places them haphazardly in various boxes like he's doling out cards for a poker game. "What next?"

"Hose nozzle." I am glad to leave the filter aisle. I have this fear that soon an employee in a red Lowe's jacket will come barreling down the aisle and tell all of us to leave.

Ryan pushes the cart back to the main aisle. He runs to the seasonal items in the middle of the store. Boxes of hose nozzles fill the shelves. I didn't know there could be so many choices. Ryan glides the cart to the shelf and stops. He studies each box carefully before he reaches in and grabs a silver metal nozzle. "This one is good," he says. "My stepdad has one like it."

The nozzle is a little pricey compared to the others, but I place it in the basket.

Ryan checks his wristwatch. "Drug court starts at three o'clock."

Drug court is a special program which selects kids based on their commitment to staying clean and sober. Each week they must check in with the judge about their progress in school and sobriety. It's important they arrive on time. "I can take you to get some gas," I say. "We'll get the gas can and you can fill up."

Ryan studies the floor like he's going to find a treasure on the linoleum. "It's okay. I'll call my dad. He isn't going to like it. He'll yell at me. But I'll just call him."

"I can do it," I insist. "I'm right here."

Ryan shakes his head and looks up at me. His hair hangs just over his eyes. "I'm okay."

"But..." I stop. It's no use arguing. He will return to his dad. He will be late to drug court and end up with infractions from his parole officer. Too many infractions and Ryan will be removed from drug court for a short sentence in detention. But all of this seems like an easier route than taking gas from the lady who helps him write poetry in detention. Insanity is defined as doing the same thing over and over and expecting different results. I know all too well that most of the time it's easier to go with insanity. It's easier to hope someone else will change than to figure out a way to change yourself. As a writer, I am caught in the insanity of submitting my novels to large, traditional publishers in New York. I have revised both of my young-adult stories, but I have yet to receive the call which will open the doors to publication. Friends who are not writers ask, "But why? Why do you continue? Isn't it horrible to get the rejections?" I try to explain the ways of rejections. I try to explain how a form letter is not so good, but a personal rejection springs hope eternal. My friends stare at me with blank faces and change the subject. I admit, at times I can sound like an addict, arguing for my next high. *Just one more submission,* I tell myself.

"See you later." Ryan gives a three-fingered wave and ambles toward Drew, who stands in the middle of the store locked in an embrace with his girl. Drew untangles himself and the three stroll out the store's back door.

I turn my cart toward the checkout register. I hope that I'll hear their voices. They'll tell me that yes, they'll take my help. But there is no sign of the boys and I finish my checkout. I head toward the parking lot, and as I open the trunk, I can't help but look around. Again, there is no boat car parked on a nearby road. As I pull out of the parking lot, I look one last time for the two boys and their loping stroll. I want to believe they are headed up the hill behind Lowe's. They will cut through the residential streets and wind their way up to the juvenile detention center where drug court takes place every Friday afternoon. I want to believe they will be on time and do their weekly check-in with the judge who, after drug court is over, will eat pizza and play games with the kids in a large conference room on the second floor of the detention center.

A few weeks ago, I taught a special workshop with only the teens involved in drug court. These teens are not detained in the detention center, and after school they step into the workshop being held in a classroom in a building behind the center. The girls wear make-up and their hair drops over their shoulders in curly waves. All of them wear fashionable clothing with pants that droop a little too low and must have taken a lot of effort to squeeze into, shirt necklines that reveal a little too much when a girl leans over. I barely recognize them as teens who, only weeks before, were serving time in the detention center.

In the workshop, I bring in white gesso and ask the kids to write down words which others have said that define them. We talk about words such as *failure, sick, druggie,* and *loser.* The kids scribble madly until their paper is filled. After the paper is covered, I set out a bottle of white gesso paint and paint brushes.

"Paint over the words," I tell them.

The kids paint furiously and no one talks. When the paper has dried, we hold up our clean white pages.

"You have a clean slate," I say. "This is your page where the positive traits and words about you will be written."

The kids smile and each one of them takes their "clean slate" home with them.

As I pull out of the Lowe's parking lot and check one more time for the two boys and their girlfriend, I think about this clean slate. I want to believe in these boys and their clean slate. I want to believe they will get where they need to go. But trust doesn't come easy.

DAD'S CRAB CAKES

From the recipe book Dad made for me when I got my first apartment

Your Grandpa Hardwick made this one while we were on vacation in Virginia in 1986. This recipe makes four servings. People usually want more. So just invite one other person or double the recipe. It tends to be expensive. Not something you can do while you entertain. You can prepare ahead, then pop into the oven for final browning after company comes. This can be a grand meal, but you might want to experiment with it before you serve it to guests or significant others.

1 cup chopped onion
¼ cup chopped celery
¼ cup chopped parsley
½ cup butter
1 cup evaporated milk
1 egg
thyme, salt, pepper to taste
2 cups crabmeat (from can okay, if fresh crab not available)
1 cup breadcrumbs
paprika
parmesan cheese

Sauté onion, celery, and parsley in a little oil. Add crabmeat and thyme, salt, and pepper. Simmer until heated through. Add breadcrumbs (or packaged stuffing), milk, lightly beaten egg. Toss well.

Shape in crab shells (or custard dishes), sprinkle with bread crumbs, parmesan, dot with butter, dust lightly with paprika.

Brown in 350-degree oven for 15 minutes.

Chuck Hardwick

ST. LOUIS SUMMER BASEBALL GAME

The night of my fortieth birthday, I wait in the lobby of St. Louis Union Station for two of my college girlfriends. It is the summer we all turn forty, our birthdays falling within weeks of each other, and I've flown back to St. Louis to celebrate. Dad and my aunt have joined us, flying in from Norfolk, and it's been a weekend full of old memories as Dad and I stroll the hallways of Union Station, reading the history of St. Louis. Dad reminiscences about the old train station, which was turned into a shopping mall with a hotel, where we are staying now, during my last years of high school. Dad and I take pictures of us sitting on an old train, side by side, each of us waving. We both post the pictures to Facebook and discuss who and how many people like the photo on each of our pages. Dad has discovered Facebook, and his status updates reflect his quick wit and love of language. My brother won't friend anyone in the family, but admits he might consider adding Dad.

During our trip Dad rented a car, and there is talk about driving out to our old suburb, Kirkwood, and taking a look around. But the late July, humid and hot St. Louis days quickly end our plans. Dad says he doesn't like the heat very much anymore, and I can't breathe with the humidity pressing on my chest. I've lived in the Pacific Northwest for over fifteen years and become too accustomed to the cool summers. I'd rather sit by the hotel's pool and in the cool air-conditioned Union Station mall then venture out on a sightseeing trip to where I used to live.

The birthday plan is to attend a Cardinals baseball game with my two college friends, and I should have gotten tickets before I arrived in St. Louis. I planned the trip in April and it's now July. But I assumed it would be easy to get tickets the day of the game. Like I often do when I wait to pay bills or get gas, I pushed the edges of how far I can go. And as in bill-paying, when a check bounces because I don't quite have the money cleared yet, or the car sputters on empty as I sit in traffic on I-5, those edges push back at me.

After lunch at a restaurant inside Union Station, I stand outside the fudge shop where the men break into song while slapping fudge across wood tables, and make multiple calls to my college friend Becky who is coming for the game. I tell her I haven't gotten tickets and ask if her husband can help us out. Becky's husband is a big sports fan and knows how to find tickets the day of the game, but this time he is able to get us only four tickets in the middle box section. My stomach churns as I tell Dad and my aunt we have four tickets instead of five. Someone will have to stay at the hotel. I have let everyone down by not getting tickets ahead of time, and I look away from the disappointment I don't want to see on their faces. My aunt quickly volunteers to stay back. She says Dad should go. It's my birthday and he should celebrate it with me.

But Dad tells me he doesn't think he can go to the game. He's had two hip surgeries and they haven't settled well on him. He tells me his hip won't take walking up and down the number of stairs we'll have to climb inside the stadium.

Feeling guilty, I promise Dad that we'll all meet up for dessert after the game. Dad brushes away my words, and later as I am getting ready, appears at my hotel room door. When I open the door, he has a large wrapped present in his hand. "Presents?" I say. "You didn't have to do presents." Dad doesn't have a lot of money, and the trip from Norfolk to St Louis was expensive. We have agreed that Dad's presence for the weekend is my present.

"I thought we should do presents before the game," Dad says. "I'm not sure what time you will be getting back."

"Okay," I say, and swallow the lump in my throat. I follow Dad back to his room and sit down at a round table. Slowly, I unwrap the newsprint. Dad has always wrapped his gifts in newspaper print, most of the time in the comic section. It's a tradition in his family, he once told my brother and me. At Christmas, I love finding the packages wrapped in *Peanuts* and *Garfield*. Dad's gifts are always fun games or later, as I get older, gadgets for my kitchen.

Slowly, I pull out a brown leather box. My fingers run over the smoothness of the backgammon set. It's the set Dad and I always played first at home and then, after he and Mom were divorced, in his apartment while eating black popcorn from brown wood salad bowls. The grease from the buttered popcorn left small traces on the small, round backgammon pieces.

"Where's the popcorn?" I joke, as I try to push back the tears clogging my throat. My hands are shaking with emotion and I hope Dad can't see.

"I think the pieces are all there," Dad says. "Why don't you check?"

I unzip the case and flip open the top. The leather cup holders are tucked neatly inside, and when I lift them, I see the small white and brown pieces.

"We have time for a game. Want to play?" Suddenly I am ten again, wanting nothing more than a good game of backgammon with Dad, who called me "the game shark" for the number of times I won at everything, Mom and my brother stopped playing games with me after awhile. But Dad always played, and sometimes, Dad won.

Dad grins and carefully lowers himself into a chair opposite me. He places his cane by his side. A large bottle of Scotch sits on the dresser, along with a glass which is half-full. I look away from it.

It's been years since we played, and neither Dad nor I can quite remember how the pieces go on the board, and we spend a few minutes trying to remember how many white pieces go on the opponent's side, and how many dark pieces. Once we think we have it right, we each take a cup and dice, and the game is on.

Swiftly, we move our pieces around the board, landing on each other's game piece, pushing each other back to the beginning again. Halfway through we realize that the pieces are all supposed to be on the end points before we begin moving them off. We adjust gears and the game slows with more jumps and captures of the opponent's side. But by the end it is obvious I am going to win.

One more roll and I have all my pieces off the table.

"I won," I say as I lean back in my chair and grin at Dad.

"Game shark," Dad says and grins back at me. His eyes, so like my own, sparkle back to me.

Dad and I pack the game away, and he tells me to have a good time at the baseball game. As I stand at the door, my eyes drift to the large bottle of Scotch on the dresser. My stomach tightens with sadness and fear.

An hour later, I meet my friends in the lobby, and together with my aunt, we head off for the game. The three of us chatter about old memories of college, stealing pizza after too many parties at a fraternity house in the late 80s, and the boys we dated. At the halftime show, the 1985 Cardinals are honored, and as they troop to the field, I can't help but think how much older they all look. My aunt leans over and says, "Isn't that the years your family lived here?"

"Yes," I say, and, something inside of me tightens as I think about Dad and how much he would have loved this moment. By the fall of 1985, Dad and Mom had filed for divorce. There were no more trial separations with Dad moving in and out of the house. Dad had permanently moved out and lived in a two-bedroom apartment on the other side of our suburban town. On fall nights, the World Series played as Dad cooked dinner for my brother, sister, and me. Whenever a homerun scored, Dad slapped his towel against the counter or stomped his feet on the thinly carpeted floor. My brother mimicked him while my sister and I danced around the room, our shouts loud and boisterous. From nearby decks and apartments, we could hear the cheers of the other Cardinal fans as we celebrated our team to a championship. It seemed much more of a party than our house.

The following summer, the divorce was finalized, and my siblings and I took our first summer trips with divorced parents. Mom's parents flew us out to San Diego, where we swam in the cold Pacific waters, visited Disneyland, the Zoo, and SeaWorld, and spent hours in the pool with our cousins. It was a trip we'd been taking since I was five, and each year our grandparents alternated between giving the trip to my aunt and uncle and parents. No one talked about my dad on that year's trip.

A few weeks later, Dad brought us to Norfolk, Virginia, to see my aunt and his dad. Dad's parents had been divorced years before I was born, but both still lived in the Norfolk area. We stayed at his dad's home, ate crab cakes, and swam in the warm Atlantic waters. Dad drove us around and showed us all the places he had lived. Hurricane Charley ripped through the area during our visit, and Dad took my brother and me out to the boardwalk, where we clung to each other as the wind raced through our hair and the rain pelted at our cheeks. Years later, that summer trip with Dad became inspiration for the first children's story I sold, and in every classroom workshop, I showed the picture of my brother and me clinging to each other on the Virginia Beach boardwalk. I talked about how it felt to travel that first summer my parents divorced, and I always found at least one kid who looked at me with a light in their eyes of complete understanding.

After the game, when we arrive back at the Union Station hotel, my girlfriends suggest they come in and we can sit in the bar and talk for awhile longer. "Sure," I say. I don't tell them my stomach has been in knots since we left the game, wondering if Dad will still be awake. Will he want to join us? And more importantly, how much has Dad had to drink, and will he slur his words, embarrass me in front of my friends? The knot tightens.

"Your dad?" my aunt says. "I think he wanted to join us. Should I go get him?"

Quickly, I tell her that I want to spend time with my college friends. It's late, and she has to get up at 4:30 a.m. for a flight. I suggest that she might want to get some sleep. I hope I'm not offending her, but I'm only here for the weekend, and this is the only night I have with my two friends. Both of them have escaped for the evening without children or husbands, and all of us want to hold onto these moments.

But my promise to Dad rings in my ears like a siren. "We'll get you after the game." It's the same feeling I've had since childhood. Even though these two college friends and I have spent more than our share of time drinking our way through fraternity-house parties, and going to bars with fake IDs, and we've each had our late nights throwing up in the dorm toilets, I don't want to go tell Dad we're back from the game. I've already done the math calculations. We left at 6:30 p.m., it's now 11:30 p.m. Dad will be half-way through the Scotch bottle by now. My shoulders tense, my stomach churns, and the joy from watching the winning game with my best friends disappears.

Underneath my tense shoulders and clenched stomach, there is something else. Something that feels like tears might start at any minute, and I won't be able to stop them. And even though I have shared with them college-boyfriend drama that brought me to my knees when that boyfriend and I broke up, I don't know how to lift the weight filling my stomach and shoulders of a secret held so long I can't even begin to find how to share it.

I want Dad to join us. He's quick witted and fun. He'd join right in our conversation and have everyone laughing. I want to tell him about the game we've just watched and the team who was honored. But I can't do it. I can't go get Dad and risk seeing him drunk and showing my friends what he looks like when he's been drinking, telling too many stories and repeating himself. And the words and shame are so deep in my stomach, I can't talk about it, so I smile brightly, the way I always did as a child. It's the smile I've used all my life, the smile that works so well to fool everyone that things are fine.

I say goodnight to my aunt. I tell her I'll be up to our room shortly, and I lead my friends to a comfortable couch, tucked into a long hallway leading to the hotel's restaurant. I don't mention Dad. I pretend that everything is fine. Dad is probably in bed. We don't want to bother him.

Forty-five minutes later, when I get back to our shared hotel room, my aunt is on the phone. "Your dad wants to know when we are getting together," she says.

My stomach clenches hard, and I feel like I might throw up the nachos and soda I had at the game. I stare at the phone she holds as if it's something foreign. But the moment doesn't last long. I'm so very good with lies and smooth moves, and this is just another moment in a long string. I quickly dump my purse on the bed and say brightly, "Oh, the game just went so long, you know. Tell him that we'll see him in the morning. I'm tired."

My aunt repeats my words and I slip into the bathroom. I stare at myself in the mirror. Who is this person who manipulates so easily? I've just turned forty, but I lie like I did when I was thirteen. A few well-polished phrases and sentences and I have managed to cover up with lies and embellishments. I'm shocked at how the words flowed out so smoothly. In my life in Seattle, I pride myself on telling the truth. But, here, tonight, I've slipped back into that girl I once was, and lying is how I survive what I don't want others to see and the things I don't want to see.

My throat feels like I swallowed rocks, and I want to sit down on the floor and bawl for days. I wanted Dad to be able to come to that after the game get-together. I wanted him to be able to celebrate with us. I wanted him to, but I can't show the truth.

I am ashamed of Dad when he's drunk.

SOMEHOW

Somehow I will find a way out of this cage
This cage that keeps me locked up inside
The cage that hides the real me.

Somehow I will make it out of this cage
Once I find myself I will be let free
Until then I will be stuck here in myself.

Somehow, something will give me the strength
To change the things I do
Whether it's the Lord or this jail cell.

Somehow I will make it out.
No more tears, I can't keep crying

No more pain, I can't keep hurting.
The cage that keeps me in myself is my own mind

I feel trapped in myself because it's all I know.

Somehow I will release myself from this cage
This cage that keeps my family in such despair.
I have to stop.
I have to free myself.
Somehow
Someway.

Because I Wanted To Be Loved, January 2009.

MISSING POETRY WORKSHOP SUPPLIES

The pink cherry trees are in bloom and the yellow daffodils planted in the garden beds lining the detention center concrete walls dance in the wind. Newspapers are stacked in blue and red bins outside the center's double doors. Colton Harris Moore's face is plastered on the front of every paper—both city and county. He lies on the ground, holds up a cell phone, and snaps a picture of himself. It's a picture which has been reprinted whenever there is a new story about Colton, who has become the Barefoot Bandit after he leaves his bare footprints in the island grocery-store floor on a midnight robbery excursion. For the past two weeks, the news has been filled with tales of Colton flying planes. He's stolen planes from hangers on Orcas Island and crashes them when he lands. Amazingly, Colton is never hurt. He walks away from the scene and leaves the planes a crumpled mess.

I lean closer to read the headlines. A small plane from Anacortes has been recovered on Orcas Island. Another grocery store has been burglarized and somebody has drawn bare footprints on the floor—Colton's signature calling card. I know this store. My mom and stepdad own property on Orcas and I visit often in the summer. The last time they visited the island, my parents discovered a small wood bench missing from their property. My parents don't have a house on the property. Instead, they take their RV and park it for months during the summer. The wood bench is the only thing they leave on the land. We have a great time discussing whether or not Colton visited their land. Did he make a fire on their rocky beach? Did he burn the bench to keep warm?

I turn away from the papers and open the double doors of the detention center. It is the lunch hour and no one is waiting outside the court room. Once I clear through security, I walk into the lobby and toward the windows. As I pull open the silver drawer and insert my driver's license, a picture of Colton Harris Moore tacked to the bulletin board, on the other side of the glass windows, stares back at me. It's his 2006 mug shot for Denney. Although the news buzzes about Colton, no one talks about him at the detention center. There seems to be an unspoken rule that he is not to be mentioned. There is only his picture plastered to the bulletin board.

I never worked with Colton during the poetry workshop, but I did spend time working with the young man who would become Colton's accomplice. The young man wrote poetry about his new baby daughter. He told me how he was going to change his life. Now, this young man's face appears on the evening news. He refuses to answer questions about Colton's whereabouts. Is his young daughter watching her dad on TV? He is older than eighteen, so his next sentence will begin in the county jail rather than Denney. Will his daughter visit him in prison?

I lean against the concrete walls and wait for the guards to open the locked doors. I've just taken my first ride in a private plane, and I can't imagine anyone learning to fly without lessons. My friend Chris spent weeks telling me about his flying lessons. He told me how he didn't pass the test the first time and he can't fly with instruments until he gets 100 flying hours. This means Chris can't fly in clouds. I asked him over and over what happens if he does run into clouds. The Seattle skies are filled with clouds most of the year. I grilled him. Does he have to land immediately? If he doesn't have instruments then how will he get out of the clouds? Chris patiently explained that, most likely, he can check for clouds before he flies. And, he said in the same calm voice, if he is in the air, and a sudden bank of clouds moves in, he'll drop below the clouds and land at the closest airport. I agreed to take a flight. But I didn't tell him how scared I was we would fly into clouds.

The day of our flight dawned bright and sunny and it turned out clouds aren't the only thing to worry about when flying. Maneuvering around other planes in the sky is a bigger concern than clouds. Chris carefully instructed me to tell him when I see another plane near us. I took my job seriously, and as soon as I saw the glimmer of silver wings on the distance, I tapped him on the arm and pointed out the window toward the plane. Chris nodded and spoke into his mouthpiece, alerting the other plane of our location. The flight was smooth and I enjoyed the afternoon of being in a space that was wide open and free of people and traffic congestion—something hard to find in the Seattle area. Maybe that's what Colton was seeking too.

Now, as I lean against the concrete wall, I fiddle with my canvas bag's strap. How long can Colton continue to crash planes before he burns?

The locked door clicks open and I step into the hallway. Today I am a part of the school day for the workshop, and the school program director, Eric, is waiting for me on the other side of the door. He apologizes for running late as we walk down the hallway to the stairs which lead up to the school classrooms. I've known Eric for more than ten years. He was on the hiring committee when I got my first teaching job. During my early years of teaching, Eric taught science across the hall. More often than not, his classes could be found engaged in a real-life experiment of putting balloons into the air or testing chemicals in small beakers. After teaching seventh grade, Eric left to work on his school-principal degree. He's spent time working with kids at the alternative high school and now works as the school program director at Denney. His hair is a little bit grayer, but his eyes still sparkle and he still has a kindhearted spirit that draws both kids and teachers to him. Eric seems to understand what I'm doing with the kids and never questions my methods or tries to control what goes on in poetry workshop. He's often a sounding board as we walk down the hall and discuss current kids housed in detention.

Eric unlocks a door that leads to a stairwell. The stairwell is one of the few places where there are no cameras watching every move. When a unit is in the stairwell, I am often told to wait until they exit out before I can enter. Today, there are only Eric, me, and two men who are working on the stairs. The men insert a metal cage which wraps around the upstairs and covers the edges of the stairs.

"What are they doing?" I ask.

Eric shrugs. "One of the kids tried to throw himself over the stairs. He didn't succeed."

I gasp and look upward. Both the stairs and the floor below are concrete. A kid trying to throw himself over the edge means one thing—suicide. Was the kid someone I knew? Was he supposed to be in the poetry workshop? I'm not allowed to ask for too much specific information about the kids, and I'm pretty sure Eric won't tell me who it was. I try not to think about it as we make our way around the men and their drills.

On the second floor, Eric leads me down the hall and into a classroom. The classrooms have regular tables which seat two students each and black plastic chairs. There are no heavy pieces of furniture like in the units. Motivational posters and class rules are plastered to the concrete walls. A teacher's desk sits in the front of the room with a computer and various baskets filled with papers and manila folders. There is a large row of windows that line one side wall where guards pace up and down the hallway while the kids are in class. Smaller windows line the top of one wall of the room. They are too high to climb out of, or to see much through, but the blue sky still peeks through the top.

I set my bag on the teacher's desk and look around for the supplies. The supplies of poetry workshop are simple: pencils and paper. The pencils in the school day are long with thick erasers on the end, and each set of twelve is stored in Styrofoam spheres. Each pencil has its own hole in the circle to ensure that once the workshop is over, every hole will be filled in that piece of Styrofoam.

Eric and I arrange the tables into a circle, and the kids' slap of their plastic sandals moves closer to us as they walk down the hallway toward the classroom.

"It's mostly kids you've had before in the workshop," Eric says as he hands me the unit's roster.

"Thanks." I appreciate the trust I'm given with the units. I could ask for a teacher to be in the room with me, but because I have maintained my current Washington State teaching certificate and Eric taught with me and trusts me, I am allowed to be a teaching artist in the room alone. The visual artist who comes once a week has a team of three who work with her, but I like the privacy of not having a guard or a teacher listen to every conversation. It seems to free the writers to share their poems at the end of the session, and gives me an insight into their lives that I suspect they wouldn't casually reveal if someone else was in the room.

The boys enter the room, and a few nod to me. Eric is right—most of them know me from previous workshops. As soon as the guard leaves to stand in the hall, the boys start joking with me and each other. Do they know the kid who tried to commit suicide? If they do, no one mentions it. I assemble my notes and books and allow the chatter and jokes. The boys let off steam as they jostle each other about girls they know on the outside, Taco Bell, and who took extra milk last night at dinner. I don't mind the chatter and jokes as long as they work, and today, after a little prompting from me suggesting we write about foods we miss in detention, this group is able to do both.

At the end of the hour, I am startled when I realize we barely have time for me to pick up the pencils before the unit needs to be lined up at the door. The rotation of moving the units through the hallway and into their other classes operates with the precision of landing planes. It's often hard for me to hustle and get the kids out the door at their scheduled moment. Nine times out of ten, someone decides, at the last minute, to share their poem with the group. I never like to cut off a poet reading, but if I am even a minute late, I mess up the rotation of the classes' passing time.

I stand up and pass the Styrofoam sphere around the table and each boy sticks his pencil into a hole. When it gets back to me, there is an empty hole.

"Alright." I place my hands on the hips and stare at the twelve boys. "Who has the pencil?"

The boys know no one walks out with a pencil. Sharp items can be used to stab.

"Not me!"

"Man, put the pencil back. I don't want to be searched."

Boys are up and out of their seats. They are under the table, they are walking around the room, and everyone is talking.

"Man, who has the pencil?"

"Count again."

"I don't want to be searched."

The classroom door flies opens and the guard stands in the doorway. A scowl is on his face and he's got his hand positioned on his belt. "What's the problem?"

"Someone stole a pencil."

"Don't search us."

"Man, 'fess up!"

The guard eyes me. "Is that right?"

I hold up the Styrofoam with the empty hole. "There is one missing," I say meekly.

Jesse kneels on his chair and looks down into the slots of the table. The tables have a small hole by the leg. I've seen pencils dropped down the leg. Usually, you can reach your hand into the table hole and pull up the pencil.

He reaches his hand into the table leg, but comes up empty-handed. "Man. Are we going to be searched?"

"Alex." The guard points to a young man who is known for being antsy and talkative. "I want to see you in the hall."

Alex stands and shakes his orange pants at the guard. "I don't have a pencil!"

"Now!" The guard snaps.

Alex drops his hands behind his orange T-shirt and counts for the guard. "One," as he walks out the door.

The room is silent. Everyone watches Alex through the windows. In the doorways of the other classes, lines of kids in orange wait to be allowed to walk through the hallway.

The guard shakes Alex's shirt and his pants. He runs his hands up and down his legs as if searching him for contraband at the airport.

"He's lucky it's not a cavity search!" Josh says.

"For a pencil?" I'm pretty good at knowing when they are making stuff up.

"We're going to be in lockdown for sure." Jesse says.

"You've got books to entertain yourselves with." I point to the paperbacks in each of their hands. These particular ones are cast-offs from either the community or the school district. I've often seen the stamps inside the paperback books. Discarded. But the poetry workshop has been able to apply for grants through the school district, and I buy young-adult novels and memoirs for the poetry workshop. The librarian places them on their own shelf marked *Poetry Workshop*. They are new books, not discarded, something both the kids and I notice and thus treat with a special reverence, making sure not to bend pages or crease covers.

"Man, I don't want to be in lockdown."

The door opens and Alex comes back from the search. He slinks to his seat. The guard shakes his head. He stares at the boys. By this point, the other units are moving past the windows. It's the end of the school day, and the kids are headed back to their units for their thirty-minute mandatory silent-reading period in their cells while the guards change shifts. Some glance over at our classroom and I see the questions in their eyes.

"Who has the pencil?" The guard crosses his hands across his chest. "We're not going anywhere until it shows up."

"Man, come on. I want a snack."

"Count them again," Alex says to me.

I pick up the Styrofoam sphere and count pencils. There are twelve pencils. I recount. Twelve pencils. I stare at the empty hole. "There are all here," I say slowly. My face flushes. I have made a big mistake. Why didn't I count the pencils before? I only looked at the Styrofoam and assumed since one was empty, a pencil was missing.

"Man, thank you!" Jesse lifts his hands to the air as if he is in church and praising God.

"But the hole…" I stare at the empty hole. How can there be twelve pencils and an empty hole? Slowly, I remember I didn't remove the Styrofoam sphere from the table. I am supposed to pass out the pencils and place the Styrofoam on the teacher's desk. At some point during the workshop, someone took the Styrofoam and punched an extra hole in it. There appears to be a pencil missing, but there is not. And because I hate the pencil-counting routine, I have only looked to see if the holes are all filled.

"I think," I say slowly. "This was my fault."

"Nah, man," Alex says. "Don't worry about it." There is a quick flurry as the boys stand, push in their chairs, and line up at the door.

The guard ushers them out and I am left holding the pencil container as Josh turns around. He smiles at me on his way out the door. "No biggie," he says. "We didn't get lockdown. See you next week."

LOVE FOR YOU

The love I hold within my soul
It's always there
It will never go
Unless it fades, there it stays
Hold me forever
Each and every day.
I love you, boy.
I really do
Can't explain how much love I've got for you
It's like a dream
I cannot sleep
There I lay and dream so deep
Wishing we could be together
Hold each other
Laugh forever
You never know what life may bring
You-n-me—that special thing.
I love you.

Please Brave Me, Dry These Tears, November 2009.

A SPECIAL KIND OF LOVE

"She wasn't a bad girl," Rene says.

The rhyming book lies open on the round table. Colorful stenciled drawings line the wall of the art room in the detention center. The guards wait outside the windows, but there is no one else in the classroom. Rene and I are working together as a part of the Blanche Miller Trust workshop. It's a special workshop, separate from the weekly poetry workshop, which is funded by the Blanche Miller Trust. Over the course of a week, I will work individually with eight writers. The format is similar to the one I use in the weekly workshop where the poetry topics are intended to encourage personal experience writing. But the individual one-hour time slot for each writer allows me to give more time to the elements of crafting a poem. We talk about techniques such as rhyme, rhythm, and repetition. I encourage the writers to do some minor revisions during the hour, shaping their poems a bit more than we do in the weekly workshops. The writers will receive community credit hours as a part of publishing their poetry in the annual poetry books, which are also funded by the Blanche Miller Trust. Usually the writers are selected by Eric or one of the other teachers who chooses kids who might benefit from extra time with me.

But this week, I have requested to work with Rene.

"No?" I say, hoping if I don't ask too much he might continue. I know the girl Rene mentions. I've gotten to know Morgan quite well in the last three months while she's awaiting sentencing. Morgan's not one of the regulars, the ones who the staff calls "the frequent flyers," kids who circulate back through the detention center over and over on different charges. For many of them, the detention center's small cells lining the concrete walls of each unit are safer than a home or their pimp's apartment.

"Nah." Rene shakes his head, and his long hair flops across his forehead. The boys don't usually have to wear rubber bands like the girls.

He continues to thumb through the rhyming book as he searches for words to fit into his poem like an elaborate jigsaw puzzle. "She was just there because of me."

I know about "just there." "Just there" is the scene of the crime. "Just there" has seeped into the detention center lobby as gang pamphlets show up in the racks and tables. Gangs have not been a problem in the suburban county of the detention center—until recently.

Rene draws a circle with his finger on the table. "Before me, she went to school. She got okay grades."

I nod. I've read about Morgan in one of the newspaper articles, too. But I've been running the poetry workshop long enough to know the details of a kid's crimes are not something to be discussed. It's a rule I've followed from the beginning and ensures that I always see the teen with a clean slate as a writer and not as their crime.

"My mom moved us up here to get away from the gangs," Rene says as he finds the word he has been looking for, and very carefully fills it into his poem. "But it didn't work." He shrugs. "They're here, too."

Renee's handwriting is precise and controlled, something that I notice in a handful of the kids' scripts. The handwriting reminds me of a letter sent from prison years ago. One Sunday at church, not long after Dad had moved out, a lady stood up and talked about a prison pen pal writing program she was leading. As she talked about the benefits to the prisoners and how safety would be ensured for those who chose to participate, I couldn't stop staring at the woman. She was tall and blond with a light around her body that drew me in. Up until that point, I'd never really thought much of church—it was somewhere to go on Sunday mornings where we colored pages of Jesus in long beards, read stories about animals walking two-by-two, and drank watered-down orange juice from plastic cups. The church we attended drew on the same group of kids at school who were popular, self-assured, and lived in the brand-new subdivision near the mall in beautiful, stately homes. Although I attended Sunday school, weekly confirmation classes, and a high-school youth group, I never found comfort in church during my parents' separation and divorce, and I silently skated the edges of every church event. I preferred to be with Dad at Church of The Old Donut Shop. But Dad had moved out and my donut option was gone.

After church that day, Mom pulled me aside and said, "I think we should sign up to write to this prisoner, don't you?'

I had agreed, fascinated by what type of letters we would receive and who this prisoner would be. But I was also fascinated by this woman and the light she carried around her body, which I saw so clearly. At the time, I never thought to question whether writing to prisoners would be a good idea for a single mom with three kids who had just left an abusive marriage, and neither did anyone else who cleared us into the program. A few weeks later, a small letter arrived with the state prison seal on it. Mom laid it out on the yellow kitchen table where she smoked her menthol cigarettes. I stared at the small, neatly printed letters handwritten carefully on the lined school paper. I don't remember much about what was in those letters or how long we wrote back to the prisoner or even what we said, but years later as I work with the kids in detention, I see the same precise, controlled handwriting in the poems they write.

Rene works on his poem and I study him, thinking about the gangs. The gangs fascinate me. In the last few months, I've skipped reading the pamphlets and instead read a couple memoirs written by former gang members, including *Always Running: LaVida Loca Gang Days in LA*, by Luis J. Rodriguez. The memoirs give me an inside understanding that helps when I'm working with the latest group of teens in detention. I've recommended a couple books to Eric and seen them appear on his shelves too.

Rene finishes his poem and hands it to me. "Is it good enough for the book?"

"Yes," I say. "Do you want a copy?"

"Yeah." Rene nods.

"Okay." I tuck the poem into my folder, and tell him that at the end of all the thirty- minute individual sessions, I will make copies of all the poems, and return them to the units. Rene stands up and pushes his chair in. "See ya," he says, and smiles shyly at me.

"See ya," I say, and watch him walk out.

I haven't told Rene that I have also picked his girlfriend, Morgan, to participate in one of the individual workshops. Morgan is a natural pick for the Blanche Miller Trust workshop. She writes well and has been at the detention center for months. She needs something to do while awaiting her sentencing. No one disagrees with me.

As I wait for the guards to bring Morgan from her unit to the classroom where I am conducting the individual workshops, I remember the first day I met Rene.

We had received a grant from Boeing Employees Credit Union which allowed me to purchase young-adult novels and memoirs and conduct a special workshop which ran in five consecutive days of one week instead of once a week the way the usual poetry workshop ran. Both Eric and I were eager to find out how reading the young-adult novels and memoirs would enhance the poetry writing experience. We also hoped that by being there for a period of five consecutive days I would have a greater chance of working with the same kids in one unit rather than returning the following week and finding half of them had been released or were no longer in that unit.

I had opened the week's workshop by showing clips from HBO's "Brave New Voices." It's a collection of poetry performed in a Poetry Slam by some of the country's most outstanding teen poets. I hoped hearing other teens speak poetry, written from the heart, would give the detention center writers more authority for their own voices.

When Rene's unit first filed into the classroom, it was hard not to miss the number of Class A felon wristbands. Usually I am not scared to be in a classroom with a group of boys wearing orange. But that day, my hand shook as I picked up the roster. I glanced up to the large classroom windows. The guard watched us intently. No one was smiling. There were more guards than usual, and a couple of them were watching two boys exclusively. These boys seemed much bigger and older than the detention center cut-off age of eighteen. Carefully, I took attendance from the roster. I didn't let my eyes stray to the right-hand column which listed the boys' crimes. I knew the boys were watching my every move. And I knew they were waiting for the fear—the fear that showed I was intimidated by them.

Quickly, and with my breath sounding a little shallow, I explained the poetry workshop. I explained how I would be working with the unit for a week, and that I was going to start by showing them the "Brave New Voices" poetry video clip.

I flipped on the computer and projector. As the boy on the screen started speaking, one of the boys suddenly leaned forward on his arms. His face changed from hardened to open and clear. His eyes widened. On the screen, the teen boy finished reading his poem, and the audience on the screen erupted into cheers; the boys in the classroom didn't move.

The video continued to play as the detention center boys laughed and clapped, a few even tapping their fingers on the table to the beat of the poems recited on the screen. A wall of sadness and frustration bubbled up inside me. Why didn't this type of poetry get to these kids before they ended up here? Traditionally, the poetry slams are targeted to the cities;

Seattle, San Francisco, D.C., and not the suburbs. But gangs and crime don't care about city boundaries, and watching the boys, I could see how much a poetry slam was needed in our suburban county.

During that week-long workshop, I also integrated novels in verse and bought copies of books by Ellen Hopkins, *Crank* and *Glass*, as well as books by Sonya Sones for the one unit of girls that participated in the workshop. As soon as I opened the box and pulled out the books, the girls clamored to read them. By the second day, they had passed them around their units like a popular drug, and over half were done with at least one. By the third day, the guard pulled me aside and said the girls didn't want to do anything but sit in their cells and read. He asked, "What exactly were these books?"

During that week, the girls' poems took on a voice I hadn't heard before. They became confident in the ability to tell their stories through poetry. They read books with characters whose stories mirrored their own and their own words flowed onto the page. It's something I understood well from my own middle-school years, when I devoured the "problem novels" of the 1980s as I searched for answers to understand my family's issues. During my MFA program, I learned they are labeled "problem" or "issue" novels, books with characters who struggle with an issue such as alcoholism, suicide, and cancer. These "issue novels" go in and out of popularity, and by the time I have written my own "issue novel" about a teen struggling to stay sober, they are no longer in favor and I have a hard time selling my book. *Weaving Magic* finally sells to a small e-publisher and I retain the print rights, something which allows me to bring the book out in print. I purchase copies at discount and mail them to treatment centers and recovery programs across the country, knowing the story will find the right audience.

"Is this the poetry class?" A soft voice pulls me out my thoughts and I look up to see Morgan enter the classroom. She is smiling and carrying her thick manila school folder. Morgan's eyes are soft and I have a hard time believing this young lady could commit a horrific crime. The detention center school staff and guards tell me she has another side, but I have not seen it.

"Hey." Morgan pulls out the same chair where Rene has just sat. She sits down. "Did you see Rene?"

I am not supposed to pass messages between Rene and Morgan. All staff is supposed to keep all communication separate from kids who are being sentenced for crimes committed together. Eric tells me the parents often pass messages between the kids, written in Spanish, in visitation. The guards don't speak Spanish.

"Maybe," I say, and smile at Morgan. It is hard not to like Morgan. She is smart and her dark eyes dart everywhere and miss nothing. She is not defiant, or resistant, and most of all, she is a great writer.

"Can I write about him?" Morgan pulls the stack of notebook paper sitting on the table toward her.

"Sure," I say. Technically, allowing Morgan to write about Rene means they are writing back and forth and I am breaking the rules. I am allowing communication between them. I am encouraging the relationship. But I also know the rules of poetry workshop—write honestly and write from the heart. If I tell Morgan not to write about Rene, then I am breaking the rules of poetry workshop.

"Will you put our poems together in the book?" Morgan asks.

"Maybe," I say. I hide my smile and doodle on my yellow tablet. I am a hopeless romantic, and there is something about this relationship which is as good as any romance story. At the time, I am working on *Weaving Magic,* and it's not filled with nearly the amount of angst, longing, and passion that I see in the poems of Morgan and Rene.

After an hour, Morgan hands me her poem. She reminds me to be sure and give her a copy. When I open the folder, Morgan leans over and touches Renee's poem. "Mmm…" she says. "He wrote one too. Can I read it?"

"No," I say, and smile at her. "But when the poems are published in our book, I'll put yours side by side, okay?"

"Okay." Morgan's bright eyes shine at me as the guard opens up the door and tells her it's time to go.

The guard eyes me a minute, as if he knows what I'm up to, then shakes his head and says nothing as he escorts Morgan out the door.

MISSPELLINGS:

My High School Story

Times she'd been in trouble: 0
Years of school: 12
Years of Life: 17
Small pink note delivered to her Independent Living class by an unsmiling student office assistant with her name and instructions to see the Senior Principal—NOW: 1
Open-walkway hallways from her Independent Living class to the office: 2
Double doors to open: 2
Boys waiting outside the office: 3
Girls waiting outside the office: 0
Vinyl red chairs in the outer waiting area: 6
Cushioned green chairs inside the office: 2
Diplomas on the wall: 3
Large deep-cherry wood desk: 1
Handwritten note with one misspelled word—Excuse: 1
Days of in-school suspension received: 5
Swim coach who advocated for her: 1
Suspension afternoons allowed at the pool where she watched her team practice: 2
Bleachers where she sat and timed practice 100 freestyles: 1
Swim meets missed: 2
500-meter swim events missed: 2
400-IM medley events missed: 2
Marlboro Light 100 cigarettes smoked on the drive home: 2

Air fresheners sprayed in the car when she pulled in the driveway: 1
Prayers she made for high school to be over: 1

**Inspired by Suzanne LaFetra's "Nine Days" published in Brevity Issue 24/Summer 200

JURY DUTY

Dear Court Clerk,
Please excuse Mindy Hardwick from
jury duty. She is needed to run a poetry
workshop with the youth at Denney
Juvenile Justice Center.
Thank you,
Mindy Hardwick

Quickly, I double check "excuse." *C after X,* I remind myself.

The word *excuse* and I have a long history together. As a high-school senior, I burned the candle on both ends: swim practice, a full load of classes, and endless phone conversations with two of my best friends. When the morning arrived, the cozy covers and warm bed called to me more than rising to face another day of high school. Every morning, I waited until the last possible second before I opened the door to our home across the street from the high school and ran across the empty street and down the grassy hill to class. It wasn't that I didn't like my first period, in fact I enjoyed Independent Living. I loved keeping a checkbook and using an imaginary budget to plan for furnishing an apartment. I couldn't wait for the day when I could live independently. I imagined it would be as much fun as the day I earned my driver's license and no longer had to depend on Mom to take me places.

During senior year, Mom's job didn't leave her time to cajole a seventeen-year-old daughter out of bed. Instead, she would call from the bottom of the stairs, "I'm leaving for work now. Are you up?" "I'm up!" I always yelled back. My brother never had a problem with early mornings and was out of the house long before I even managed to open an eye. My sister went with Mom to be dropped off at an early-morning childcare program, and I was left alone in the house. After I heard Mom's car leave, I dragged myself out of bed and toward the bathroom to get ready for school. This usually worked fine, until one morning when I fell back asleep. By the time I woke up, the cars at the high-school parking lot were all in their spots and the school was quiet.

The only way for me to get into school on an excused pass was to write a note—using Mom's handwriting. Mom always used the same thick blue stationery paper with her initials on the top. She'd been using the stationery for as long as I could remember to sign me out for doctor's appointments and orthodontist appointments and excuse me when I was sick. The morning I overslept, I simply got up, went to Mom's top desk drawer and pulled out her blue stationery.

Please ecxuse Mindy Hardwick from her first-period class. She had a dentist appointment.

At the bottom of the paper, I scrawled Mom's signature. I'd been practicing her signature for weeks, knowing there might come a day when I would need it. By senior year, it seemed to be harder and harder for me to get up in the morning. I loved nighttime, after my homework was finished and all my phone calls done. The world belonged to me and I could spend hours reading whatever book I wanted, not the books my teachers insisted I read. I devoured books by Danielle Steele and Barbara Taylor Bradford, long family sagas that took me out of my own world and into elaborate, stately homes with family dynasties that stretched over multiple books.

I savored those late hours when everything became still and quiet outside my window and I finally had the freedom I craved to do whatever I wanted and not what my teachers, coaches, and friends wanted me to do. My room was tucked away in the far end of the house, upstairs and away from Mom's room. Mom, my brother, and sister all liked to go to bed early. Dad had been the one to stay up late, smoking his pipe, watching TV, and taking the dog for a late-night walk at the high school. Years later, my friends would tell me the one thing they remember about Dad is how he used to walk the dog around the perimeter of the high school late at night. But in those late-night walks, Dad always knew if my lights were on because he could see them shining from my windows.

In the school office, I handed my note to the secretary. I smiled and waited for the green pass. I don't remember if the secretary looked at the note any differently. I don't remember her holding the note up to the light. I don't remember her asking me to sign my mom's name to check the signatures. But I do remember there was a pause, much longer than there should have been. Something in my stomach tightened, but I took the green pass and headed off to second period.

An hour later, a student runner brought a pink pass with my name on it, summoning me to Dr. Faulk's office. Dr. Faulk was one of the vice principals of the senior class, and it fell to him to take the disciplinary action. It wasn't the first time I'd been to see him. In the fall, Mom and I made a visit to his office to request a leave of absence so I could attend my brother's treatment family week. Dr. Faulk told us I could have a week of vacation while Mom sputtered beside me. "Family week at her brother's rehab is *not* a vacation. She is learning about the disease of alcoholism."

I expected no more compassion on this trip to his office than the one in the fall.

When I arrived in Dr. Faulk's office, Jeffrey Dell lounged on a plastic chair in the waiting room. He gave me a sexy smile. "How's it going?"

"It's going," I plopped down in the chair next to him. Jeffrey and I had gone to school together since fourth grade. For as long as I could remember, Jeffrey was always in trouble. I had only been in trouble once— during middle school. I'd been part of a group of three girls who wrote mean notes about another girl and stuck them under our desks for someone else to find. Our teachers recognized the handwriting and we were all hauled in to a four-teacher team meeting to talk about the problems. I had done things which should have gotten me in trouble, like charging jeans on Mom's credit card, but I had never been in trouble in school since that fateful day in middle school. I was too scared to do anything that might draw attention to me and force the secret of our family's brokenness to the light.

On that day in Dr. Faulk's office, I asked myself: Why was I sitting with Jeffrey, who was always bad? I wasn't bad. Okay, I admitted, I wrote a note and signed my mom's signature. But that wasn't that bad, was it? I clutched my Gucci purse closer to me as if it would prove that I was one of the good girls, the popular girls who did not get in trouble. I had bought the hundred-dollar purse with my first paycheck from my summer job at Six Flags over Mid-America, where I worked in the games department. The past winter, I had been promoted to an assistant foreman. My new job involved replenishing everyone's quarter tills, checking on water for the hot, humid evenings, and assigning each person a games stand for their shift. I'd been chosen as employee of the month and wore a gold name badge on my red-and-white Britannica uniform. I loved my job at Six Flags, where everyone came from high schools all over the St. Louis area. The cliques I'd been forced to confront in my high school where I never fit in dissolved at Six Flags. We all formed new cliques based on the area of the park where we worked. Those of us who worked in the games department were on the top of the clique order. We were known to be the ones who had the most fun, the best parties, and were some of the smartest workers as cash streamed through our hands nightly. I loved my job. I was well-liked and well-respected. I was not someone who got in trouble.

My stomach churned as I waited for my name to be called. I had always had a nervous stomach. A few years earlier, on my first real date, I was so nervous, I couldn't eat and had to take my entire meal home in a take-out box. My date never questioned it, but Dad did as soon as he saw us step out of the restaurant. Dad acted as our chauffer and had driven my date and me in my grandparents' car to the local Italian restaurant where everyone went before the annual fall dance. Grandma and Grandpa traveled extensively, and they often left their car at our home while they flew out of the St. Louis airport. It was one of the earliest Chrysler Town Cars to have a voice-activated command system, and Dad couldn't wait to show off my grandparents' toy. After we picked up my date, Dad posed both of us outside the restaurant and snapped pictures. The boyfriend didn't last beyond the one dance, and after getting my first sloppy and wet kiss at the door, I didn't want him to see him again anyway. I was pretty sure Dad had more fun on that date than I did.

"Mindy Hardwick." Dr. Faulk's deep voice rang out from his office.

"Good luck." Jeffrey saluted me and winked.

I stepped into the small office and sat down in a heavy wood chair across from a matching desk.

Dr. Faulk did not greet me. He did not smile at me. He did not show any recognition that he knew me from the request to have a week's leave to attend my brother's family week in rehab. Instead, he glared at me from over his glasses. "Do you know why we called you in?"

"I forged a note." I wasn't going to lie.

"Do you know how we know?"

I shrugged. I didn't really care how they knew. They knew.

"Do you see how *excuse* is spelled?" Dr. Faulk pushed my note toward me. I stared at Mom's pretty blue stationery paper with my handwriting. *Excuse* looked fine to me.

"There is a c after the x." Dr. Faulk yanked the note back. He reached up to a bookcase next to him and pulled out a tall stack of papers with carbon copies.

I crossed my hands over my chest. I was a senior in the spring of my senior year. I had a B average. I was already accepted to college and I had never been in trouble in high school. We were talking about skipping one class, which was an elective class. It wasn't math. It wasn't English. It wasn't science. It was an elective. I was beginning to get a little pissed off.

"You know" Dr. Faulk looked up at me, his pen poised over the stack of carbon papers, "there is going to be a paper trail that is going to follow you."

"A what?" I couldn't believe what I was hearing. How would a paper trail follow me for misspelling *excuse*?

"There will be a paper trail." He nodded smugly at me. "That trail will follow you for the rest of your life."

Years later, each time my name appeared in print for articles or short stories, or the newspapers wrote up my upcoming author appearances or workshops, Mom called me and gleefully said, "There's the paper trail, Mindy!"

But I couldn't see the future in that moment of sitting in the office. I couldn't see that I wasn't a bad kid or that I would later run a poetry workshop with kids who had committed crimes and were labeled bad kids themselves. I only knew Dr. Faulk had just told me something that didn't seem to be reasonable, but I also couldn't find my voice to tell him that I disagreed. He was the vice principal and I was a bad student.

"I'm giving you five days of in-school suspension." Dr. Faulk leaned forward and eyed me with his beady, dark eyes.

I clung to the edges of the chair. Five days for misspelling *excuse*. Five days for a girl who had never been in trouble. It seemed more than a little unfair. But I knew that to speak up would land me in even more trouble. I had learned that lesson well with Dad at the dinner table on Saturday nights.

Dr. Faulk handed me a pink copy of the in-school suspension notice. I didn't know what I was supposed to do with it. The only thing I knew was in-school suspension met after school in the cafeteria. I had often seen the "bad" students sitting at the large white cafeteria tables as I walked by on my way home.

"Excuse me," I said quietly. "I'm in swim season. I need to go to practice." If I didn't go to swim practice, I couldn't swim in the upcoming meet. I wasn't a big competitor on the team. Most often, I swam the 500 freestyle and came in fifth or sixth. But I enjoyed swim team. I had been on the team since freshman year. I loved wearing my red-and-white sweat-suit jacket and sweatpants to school on swim-meet days. It wasn't as cool as the red-and-white pom-pom skirts and sweaters the popular girls wore, but the swim team sweat-suit said, I belong here too. Now I would belong to the bad kids in the school cafeteria.

Dr. Faulk raised an eyebrow at me. "Maybe you should have thought of that before you wrote the note."

When I walked out of the office, Jeffrey leaned against the wall, his head tilted backward and his feet outstretched in front of him.

"What'd you get?"

"Five days." I waved the pink paper in the air.

"Harsh." Jeffrey shook his head.

Harsh, I muttered as I walked down the hall and back to my class.

That afternoon, I headed for the cafeteria to serve my first day of after-school suspension. The loud room was filled with kids who had been in trouble for years. Kids who talked back to teachers, kids who didn't show up to school for weeks, and kids who hung out in the smoking area before and after school and who I knew to be my brother's drug clients. These were the kids who had troubled family lives with divorced parents and alcoholism. One part of me knew their family lives were really not much different from my own, but they didn't cover up the way I did. And now here I was for everyone to see. I was one of them.

I sat down at the round table by myself and pulled out my homework. As the afternoon wore on, I felt myself taking on the attitude of *who cares and why bother.* The attitude seeped into and permeated the room. I questioned the logic of placing all the "bad kids" together. It seemed that everyone just fed off everyone else's hopelessness. There was no teacher, only a monitor at the front of the room. No one tried to talk or work with any of us. By the second hour of the suspension, I gave up trying to do homework and stretched my legs out on the chair in front of me, daring the monitor to tell me to take them off. I'd also assumed my *I'm pissed* look, just like the attitude of the others in the room. It was a side of myself I'd never shown at school. Although I had taken up smoking, I would never light up in the school smoking area. I never went to the high-school parties and got drunk. I was too petrified to drink after years of twelve-step meeting philosophy ringing from every corner of my house. I did exactly what everyone asked me to do. But I still had that other side, the side that was angry Dad left, the side that was angry at Mom for dating this new guy whom she met in the recovery group, and all of that anger meant I could be as badass as anyone else. And sitting in that cafeteria, that other side came out full force. Wasn't that what they expected of us anyway?

I made it through that first day and prepared myself for a long week. But on the second day, before I was to report to in-school suspension, I received pink note from Dr. Faulk: *Go to the pool. Do not go to detention.* My swim coach must have had words with Dr. Faulk. I could imagine her saying, "Mindy can sit at the pool. I'll have something for her to do." A tangle of stopwatches hung from around Mrs. Smith's neck and she could always find a job for someone as a timer.

That second day of in-school suspension, I reported to swim practice. I did not get dressed in my suit, and instead sat on the steel bleachers of the humid, murky pool and watched my teammates swim. I helped Mrs. Smith time some of the sprints, but for the most part I just sat. No one asked me why I was sitting out, and Mrs. Smith didn't say anything to me about my suspension. But that feeling of being a bad kid disappeared. I was a member of the swim team who just couldn't swim for the week. On the bleachers, I was no different from a girl who had cramps and didn't want to swim for the day. I was a girl who needed a time-out, not a punishment. And years later, when I enter the juvenile detention center armed with my canvas bag slung over my back, with poetry books, a yellow tablet of paper, and a smile, that girl who needed a time-out will always be with me.

PART I

Fathers

Fathers love their kids
Fathers should never hurt their kids
Fathers should always be there for their kids
Fathers should never lie to their kids
Fathers should help learn right from wrong.

PART II

Me As A Father

Dear Son,

    I love you and I do not want you to go through the things that I went through. I have done a lot of things in my life that are not the best things to do.

    So, I promise to help you through all the hard times if you promise to let me help you through the problems.

Love,
Your Dad

Call It Courage, August 2006

POETRY IS IMPORTANT

"Got a cigarette?" A boy wearing baggy jeans and a hoodie lurks outside the detention center. The rain pours off the roof and, because this is the Pacific Northwest, none of us carry umbrellas—we can always tell a tourist as they whip out their umbrellas while we only pull up a hooded jacket.

"Sorry," I say. It's been years since I've smoked. I had picked up smoking while working at Six Flags. I worked the night shift, and on weekends attended hotel-room parties where pink wine coolers and beer were passed around like soda. My brother's drug treatment program had warned me of the likelihood of having an alcohol problem myself, so I was leery of picking up too many drinks. But I didn't want to be seen as a goodie-goodie at the parties and started smoking Marlboro Lights 100s. I figured since Mom smoked, she would never smell it on me.

"Can't even help a kid out who is going to jail," the boy mutters.

I smile at him and pull open the double doors. The boy quickly steps up to me and holds the door open. I don't recognize this boy in his street clothes, but I smile at him. "Thank you."

The lobby of the detention center is packed with waiting families, lawyers, and teens outside the court room. I place my bag on the belt and take off my belt buckle. In the time it takes me to put back on my belt, pick up my bag and scoop my driver's license out of the plastic bin on the counter, the young man is already through security.

The boy lopes in front of me into the lobby. He waits behind me as I open up the silver drawer and slip my driver's license inside before

MINDY HARDWICK   120

pushing it to the guard on the other side of the heavy glass.

Today, I am given a "Professional" plastic badge and clip it to my shirt.

I step out of the way as the young man steps forward. He speaks into the small box: "I'd like to turn myself in."

I take a sharp breath. I've never witnessed a kid turn himself in, and I marvel at his courage. Many of the teens in the poetry workshop are serving time for drug-related crimes—selling and possession. These are the teens most likely to cycle back through the detention center again and again as they battle drug addictions. Some will be assigned drug court. They will live at home and attend weekly AA and NA Meetings, volunteer time in the community, and attend school. Drug court kids must also attend a weekly check-in on Friday afternoons. Each kid shows up with their parent and talks to the judge about their progress of the week. It's a successful program and most teens want to be a part of it. But sometimes, like a go-to-jail card in the game of Monopoly, a dirty urine analysis will send a kid back to detention.

Once the locked doors open to let me in, Eric stands on the other end. He sticks his hands in his pockets and grins at me like a kid who did something wrong.

I steel myself.

"So," Eric says slowly, "I've asked Anne Marie to be in the room with you today."

"Oh?" I say, hoping he will give me more information about why Anne Marie is going to be with us today. It's not that I don't like Anne Marie, who works in the library and works as a monitor. But having another adult in the room disrupts the flow of our process.

Eric says allowing another educator to sit in on the workshop is a good way for the teachers to have professional development. I should be flattered that I am being used as a mentor teacher, and I try to be agreeable to our visitors. The English teacher watched us and then incorporated poetry into her classroom after her visit. But another time, Eric asked a popular teacher to sit in with us. During the hour she was in the room, the kids chatted with her instead of writing.

Eric tells me the classrooms are being used for individual testing and consulting and the only room open is the library. I try to be agreeable and tell him everything will be fine. I'm not sure it will be, but I try to think on the bright side.

As I am led into the library, I nod to Anne Marie. She greets me and turns back to the computer to finish an email.

Eric opens a locked cabinet and pulls out a stack of unopened lined paper along with a small Styrofoam circle with the pencils. Anne Marie reminds me that it is very important to have twelve pencils when we are finished with the workshop. "We don't want the kids to slip a pencil into their sock and later stab someone with it!"

"Yes," I say. I don't mention that I've already had the pencil test with the kids and we failed miserably.

"The rules are on the wall," Anne Marie says. "Do you want to go over them with the kids, or will I?"

I follow her pointing finger to a small, laminated white sign which hangs above the schoolroom clock. Every classroom I have ever taught in has the same clock. During daylight-savings time, the clocks are always behind or ahead an hour for weeks.

I read through the sign:

No profanity.
No talking about crimes.
Be respectful.

The rules are simple. I understand the rules, and the poetry workshop has its rules. But it's the profanity rule that is the most challenging for me. I tell the kids that there should be no profanity in their poems. I explain to them that poems loaded with profanity are automatically discarded from the publication of the yearly poetry book. I explain the books go to schools and libraries and it's not appropriate to have profanity in their poems.

But I also understand profanity is a part of the kids' lives. *Shit* and *damn* are as normal to them as *darn*. So often I hear them talk and they're not even aware they've just sworn. In the poetry workshop, I fudge the profanity rule. If a teen has written a poem which includes the word *shit* or *damn*, I don't make a big deal out of it. If the poem makes it through the release form process, I simply edit out the word before we publish. The writers and I seem to have reached an understanding of the practical realities of the rule. But I'm not sure how to work around it in a classroom with another educator.

I set out our latest copies of poetry books and hear the *click, click, click* of the plastic sandals as the kids move down the hallway. The kids wait at the door until Anne Marie tells them they can enter. This is something I always forget to do in the poetry workshop, and the guard usually has to give the command.

I spot Josh immediately as the unit enters and drops the manila folders each is holding in the wire basket at the front desk. Josh is in drug court and I've enjoyed watching his progress. When I first met Josh, his eyes were cloudy. Now, with a couple months of sobriety, his blue eyes are bright and clear. Josh works at staying sober, and has been serving time for a past sentence the last couple weeks. He writes thoughtful poetry when he's on the units, and often has a new poem to show me.

As Josh files past me, I ask, "Did you finish your poem from last week?" Josh's girlfriend just had a baby girl, and he wants to write about his new daughter, whom he hasn't seen yet. Last week we ran out of time and I told him he could take the poem back to his unit and give it to me this week.

"I've got the poem." Josh smiles at me. "I've been working on it a lot!"

"No talking!" Anne Marie snaps at us. "See that sign up there." She points to the sign on the wall.

"It was my fault," I say. "Sorry about that."

"It's his fault," she insists. "He knows the rules."

"Sorry," I mouth to Josh. I feel like both of us are sixteen and cruising for a bruising, a phrase my Dad liked to tell me a lot during my early teen years.

"It's okay," he mouths back to me.

I am always humbled by how the boys in detention never let me take the blame. Instead, they pick it up easily as if taking the fall is something they are so familiar with, they never question who might really be at fault.

Anne Marie picks up the roster and calls out names. I shift uneasily. The kids look at her, and then look at me. I understand their confusion. Who is teaching this class? Usually it is me who handles the roster. I take attendance, and then assign the points in their manila folders at the end of class. Ninety-nine percent of the time, everyone gets the full two points. The points are important to the kids. They help determine what level the kids are on in their units, and what privileges they have. I believe if you show up at poetry workshop, you get a two. Poetry workshop is not easy.

Anne Marie sets the roster aside and turns to me. She doesn't say a word.

I am nervous and feel like I am on a stage I never wanted to be on. I shift back and forth, grateful to my winter boots for grounding me into the linoleum floor. I clear my throat and pick up one of the poetry chapbooks. I flip open to a random page and start to read. It's how I open every poetry workshop. I read poems from our published book. This sets the tone. It helps kids know that other kids just like them have written poetry from the heart and it helps shift all of us into a place of honest, open sharing. But today, I know I am tense. I can hear it in my voice. I can feel the tension as it creeps up my shoulders. I don't want any more of the kids to get in trouble for talking out, but I am not sure how to negotiate this territory with Anne Marie. During workshop, I allow the kids to comment on poems we read. Sometimes they raise their hands, and sometimes they don't. As long as the room doesn't get too loud and boisterous, I allow the free flow of conversation. Anne Marie is not going to allow this type of conversation.

Josh sits in the front chair directly in front of me. He listens intently, and as I finish reading a poem about fathers, his hand snakes out for his manila folder on the front desk. Each student carries a manila folder. Inside the front cover are school papers, drawings they've completed in downtime on the units, and poems they want me to read. On the left-hand side of the folder, the tally of their school points for the day trails down the page. I can always tell how long a kid has been in detention by the shape of their folder and the tally going down the side. Some kids have two folders tucked into each other for strength. Others have brand-new folders with only one or two days marked off in points. Josh's folder has two, and it bulges with his poems and notebook paper.

As Josh's hand snakes forward, I hear a loud "Don't!" I half expect a ruler to snap down on his hand.

Josh yanks his hand back in surprise. "I just need to get my poem," he explains, while looking first at me and then at Anne Marie. The kids aren't supposed to be out of their chairs during class, and the guards keep a close eye on them from hallways windows, checking to be sure everyone stays in their seats. But when a writer needs their manila folder, and I am not available to get it immediately, they often maneuver by leaning over tables to grab the folder. I look the other way when this happens and most of the guards do, too.

I shut the poetry book and grab Josh's folder. "He just needs to get a poem."

"I'm trying to keep order for you," Anne Marie replies. Her tone tells me she thinks I am not keeping order.

I take deep yoga breaths and hand Josh his folder.

Quickly, he pulls a poem out of the top. "Can you read this one for me?"

"Sure." The other boys are silent around us. They have heard Josh's poetry and they know it's good.

I clear my throat and read Josh's poem. When I finish, a boy sitting at the back of the room says, "That was good, man."

"Yeah." A couple more kids chime in. "It's good. It should be in the book."

"That was very good, "Anne Marie says from behind me.

"Shall we write about fathers this week?" I ask, relieved that Anne Marie is not criticizing the talking out of turn.

The boys don't need much prompting. As they write, Anne Marie thumbs through the pages of the poetry book. I place my hands behind me and lean against an old wood teacher desk. It's the same type of desk I used as a seventh-grade teacher. Names and scratches are etched on the top, along the desk legs, and underneath its belly. I run my fingers along the cracks and grooves of the marks etched in the desk. What's this desk's history? Where did it come from? Was it always a part of the detention center school classroom? What sentenced this desk to days in a concrete classroom with small windows so high none of us can see anything more than barren branches on tree tops?

Suddenly, Josh looks up and stares intently at me. "Poetry is important."

Startled, I study him, wondering what he is telling me. Does he see the conflict with Anne Marie? Is he trying to tell me to relax and not to worry?

"Shh…" Anne Marie says from behind me.

"Yes," I say to Josh, not caring if Anne Marie doesn't understand the poetry workshop. "Poetry is important."

WHERE'S THE FISH?

From Dad's Blog: www.asinglemanskitchen.blogspot. com

December 2, 2011
The thought of cooking fish in a dishwasher appalled a cookbook editor, but it works, and it's fun. The idea came from a single friend who thought my children would enjoy this preparation and be inclined to eat more seafood. He used salmon, which I do not like; salmon has a strong aroma as it cooks, so he suggested running the dishwasher empty after cooking the fish. (I prefer a nice white fish like cod, or maybe even catfish.) When guests arrive, they can smell fish cooking, and hear the dishwasher running, but can't find the fish. Tim Allen devoted an entire episode of "Home Improvement" to his attempts at dishwasher fish. All failed, of course. But this won't.

firm fish fillets (one per person)
paprika
freshly ground black pepper
parsley
lemon slices

Lay the fillets on pieces of aluminum foil; add seasonings (or those of your choice).

Arrange lemon slices on top of fillets.

Wrap fillets tightly in aluminum foil and place on top rack.

Place serving dishes in bottom rack.

Run dishwasher full cycle, with hot water and the heat cycle (but no soap).

Serve on warm plates.

Chuck Hardwick

COOKING DISHWASHER FISH WITH DAD

On a rainy night in early November, Dad's small, silver, rented Toyota pulls into my driveway. I breathe a large sigh of relief. For the last five days, my brother, sister, and I have sent numerous emails coordinating Dad's drive up and down five hundred miles of the I-5 highway that goes through Oregon and Washington State. His visit is a one-week trip to see each of us for a forty-eight-hour period.

The last email I received was two hours ago from my sister. My sister tells me Dad just left her house. She lives twenty miles from Mom, but after twenty-five years of divorce, Mom and Dad have long stopped speaking to each other. None of us worry there will be a detour on Dad's trip to see Mom. It takes two hours to travel between my sister and me. Dad is right on time.

Rain pours down my windows and a light breeze blows the trees behind my deck. My house sits on a bluff above the lake, and as dark descends, the house lights shining across the lake twinkle in the misty late-fall rain. Amtrak runs between the three of us, but Dad won't take the train. He insists on renting a car and driving to each of us on his week trip. We've all explained traffic can be horrible, it gets dark early, and it rains all the time. But Dad is not going to be persuaded. He is driving to see each of us.

Dad has one goal on this trip. He wants to cook a meal with each of us. He's recently taken a cookbook writing class at the writing center near him. As a part of the class, he keeps a blog, recording his recipes and stories with each recipe. He tells each of us he will post the recipes he cooks with us on the blog.

I have requested that Dad and I make dishwasher fish. As a child, I loved cooking with Dad. He helped me earn more than one Girl Scout badge, cutting up green peppers, learning to read recipes, and helping him cook his own recipe of spaghetti. A few days before his arrival, I've gathered the ingredients. There aren't many: Tinfoil. Lemon. Seasonings. Salmon. The most important is that my dishwasher has a hot cycle. We spend a lot of time discussing my dishwasher in the weeks before he arrives.

As Dad gets out of the car, my eyes well up like they always have since Mom and Dad were divorced. I always try to hide the tears from Dad with a quick smile, or a fast blink of my eyes. Sometimes I tell him my contact is causing problems or allergies are bothering me. Dad never tells me if he believes me or not.

Once Dad is settled into the guestroom, he returns to the kitchen with a Costco bottle of Scotch. My brother says Costco-size bottles of Scotch don't travel well on Amtrak. Dad's bottle of Scotch was once stored in the sideboard cabinet, and now travels with him when he visits us. The last time Dad stayed with me, four years ago, he kept returning to the guestroom to refill his glass. This time, he leaves the bottle on the kitchen counter.

Dad takes his Scotch and walks into the living room, where he sits down in my large green chair. My calico cat, Cleo, hops up beside him. She sniffs at his drink. Dad shoos her face out of his glass. Cleo hisses at him and sticks her nose back in his glass. Dad swats her. Cleo gives Dad another hiss and a swat with her paw before leaping off the chair. "Well," Dad says, "she's quite a cat."

I hide my smile.

After three glasses of Scotch for Dad and a can of soda for me, I finally say, "Should we get started on dinner?" My stomach is churning like it used to as a child. Even though I'm an adult, and it's my house, a part of me still has that fear that when Dad drinks too much the angry words and episodes in the bathroom with the orange Dial-soap bar will happen. It's not a reasonable or rational fear, but my stomach is still locked at age eleven and not age forty-one.

"It's still early," Dad says. "What's the rush?"

"I like to eat before seven p.m." I hold Dad's gaze steady. I'm not twelve, and I've learned to hold my own. The battle between Dad, me, and his drinking has been reduced in size to a manageable conversation.

"Okay." Dad takes a long swallow of his drink as if he's swallowing the rest of what he wants to tell me. He lifts himself off the chair and balances himself in standing position. Dad's right shoe has a two-inch sole in order to balance his hips after a mangled hip surgery left him with an imbalanced left side. Dad tells all of us how the hip sets off the airport security and they have to use the wand. I tell him it's not much different from the detention center scanner that I must pass every week. Dad smiles at me and tells me again how proud he is of the work I'm doing. We've shared stories about his work as a court mediator working with families getting divorced and my work with the kids in detention. I've sent him copies of the poetry books for the mediators who work with the teens, and he always tells me they are very well read. In the last ten years, since Dad has become a court mediator, he works hard on his relationship with my brother, sister, and me. Holiday presents and cards arrive on time, phone calls are frequent, and he takes a couple visits to the Pacific Northwest to see us. It's something all of us mention to each other often.

"We'll need a few spices," Dad says. He places his glass of Scotch on the kitchen counter. The ice shifts and moves in the glass. As a child, I listened for how many times Dad refilled his glass by how many times the ice hit the edges. It's an old habit to break, and one I find myself doing at parties and social gatherings with friends. Tonight I know Dad is on his fourth drink.

"In the lower cabinet." I point to a cabinet located near Dad. Then I pull out the salmon from the refrigerator and a roll of foil from a drawer.

I hand Dad a green-and-yellow-striped apron. I bought the apron with a gift card he sent me last Christmas. Dad has discovered Amazon gift cards and I have a good time spending them, mostly on items for my kitchen. Dad slips on the apron and looks at me over his wire-rimmed glasses. "Ready to cook." He rubs his hands together.

I grin. Dad's hair is grey and he's thinner, but the twinkle in his eye is still the same. Suddenly I am that twelve-year-old girl spending time in the kitchen with Dad, and it feels as if a part of myself I didn't realize was missing clicks into place. It's always been this way. There is always a moment in the reunion with Dad where something clicks into place and I come home again.

Dad lays out the fish on sheets of tinfoil. With a scientist's precision, he spices the salmon.

"Do you want to help?" Dad holds out the pepper.

"It's okay," I say, "you can do it." I'm enjoying watching him cook. For years, I've eaten meals with Mom, and although I love Mom's soups and canned goods, I miss Dad's flair and passion. Dad gave me one of my first cookbooks—a white binder filled with plastic pages of all the recipes we cooked together. Included in that binder is dishwasher fish, but I've never been brave enough to try it on my own.

"What are we having for a side?" Dad asks.

I whip around and grab a box of yellow Rice-A-Roni from the counter. I wave the box in the air. The rice rattles.

"Of course," Dad says.

Rice-A-Roni has been a favorite of mine since I was a child. As long as we had yellow Rice-A-Roni, I could tolerate any meal. I loved to watch Dad cook dishwasher fish. He acted like a chef on a TV show, rolling up his sleeves and carefully seasoning and wrapping each piece of fish into aluminum foil. But the actual eating of it was something else. It's only been since I've lived in the Pacific Northwest that I've learned to appreciate fish.

At my kitchen counter, Dad finishes seasoning the salmon and wraps the tinfoil around it. He folds the edges into tight balls. "It's very important to enclose the fish so no water gets in." Dad's teaching voice is as familiar as my own.

Once the fish is wrapped, Dad pulls open the dishwasher and places the packages on the top rack. The dishwasher is empty. With a large flourish, Dad shuts the door and seals the latch.

"Hot cycle?" Dad stares at the controls on the dishwasher.

"It's on there," I say.

I step beside Dad and study the dishwasher. I've never really paid attention to the control buttons. I just hit *normal cycle* and don't worry about the rest. But it must have a hot cycle. Don't all dishwashers have a hot cycle?

Both of us look at the controls as if we are trying to decipher a foreign language. There is no hot cycle.

"How about normal cycle?" I say.

"Okay," Dad says. "Let's give it a try. An hour is what we want to cook the fish."

I push the button and the dishwasher hums to life.

An hour later, the dishwasher is still going and shows no sign of stopping. Dad has had a few more glasses of Scotch and I'm quickly losing my patience. I hear years of twelve-step- meeting advice in my head. "Don't get too hungry, angry, lonely, or tired."

I yank open the dishwasher and grab two hot pads. Ignoring the rising steam, I pull out the fish and place it on the granite countertop. I grab the second fish and place it beside the first.

I scoop heaping spoonfuls of Rice-A-Roni onto our plates.

"Take it easy," Dad tells me. His voice is the same controlled, precise one which used to set me off at the dinner table.

"I'm fine," I snap. "Let's just eat." I bite my tongue. I do not want to fight with Dad. Our time is limited and I don't want it filled with arguments. During his last visit, we got into an argument over cooking Cornish hens. I wanted to serve the hens to Dad, but I didn't thaw the hens well enough and ended up getting frustrated when they weren't thawing under hot water. It ruined the dinner for me, although Dad ate his hen as if nothing had been said earlier.

Dad sets the wrapped salmon on our plates and we carry the plates to the dining room table.

Carefully, I unwrap the tinfoil. My mouth waters and I carve off a bit of salmon. It flakes under my fork into tiny pieces. I take a bite. "Mmm…"

"How is the Rice-A-Roni?" Dad jabs his fork toward me.

"I'm sure it's good, too." I take another bite of salmon. "But the dishwasher fish is the best."

Tomorrow night, Dad will drive to Portland, where he will board the plane for home, his mission to cook with each of his children accomplished. For weeks, my brother, sister, and I will talk about our individual time with Dad. We will talk about our worries, our fears, and our concerns about Dad's health. We will share the little things about Dad, how he drove up and down the I-5 corridor, how he drove far out into the woods to see both my siblings who love their privacy in the woods, even though Dad hates the woods. We will talk about Dad's humor and wit, which we all love. We will talk about the pieces of Dad each of us has in ourselves. The pieces of ourselves which we forget until we see Dad and we are reminded by the mirror he holds up. We will talk about it all, but none of us will talk about how it feels when Dad says goodbye. And none of us will realize Dad has said his final goodbye to us, giving each of us a last memory of cooking with him.

MY NAME IS POWERLESS

My name is Powerless
I live in a corner
In a broken house
My last name is Fear
My middle is Doubt
My parent is Addiction
My sister is Revenge
My brother is Fury,
They go to no end.
My eyes are empty
I have no heart or soul
Knowing me really takes a toll
You won't be able to fight me
Once I've been around
Soon you meet the whole family
We'll drive you in the ground
You'll learn not to ask questions
Soon you'll be like me
Powerless has no end
Good luck getting free.

Please Brave Me Dry These Tears, November 2009.

THE DEAD BODY ON THE ROAD

The news is filled with reports of a dead body found on the side of the road. I listen to the news reports like someone staring at an accident who can't look away. I drive over this road every week on the way to the detention center. By midday, the reports say it is a body of a fifteen-year-old girl. She's been hit by an unidentified hit-and-run driver. The police are looking for the driver. I fire off emails to my teacher friends. Do they know this girl? Was she a student in their classes? The responses trickle back to me and no one seems to know her.

That afternoon, when I drive to the detention center, yellow tape marks the spot in the road where the girl died. I grip the steering wheel and stare straight ahead. I don't want to see if there is still a spot of blood.

After I am cleared through security, a guard walks me down the hall. I wonder if he knew her, but nothing is said. During my years of classroom teaching, we had workshops on grief. "Everyone handles grief differently," the facilitator told us. Some people will want to talk about it, others will want to take actions and some will want to pretend it didn't happen. The workshop leader told us it's good to know how you process grief so you can tell people beforehand and they will respect your wishes. At the time, I wasn't sure how I acted in grief. I hadn't had a death in my family since I was seven when a great-grandmother died, and I'd never lost a close friend or student. I'd grieved passages in my life, but somehow I think this type of grief is different from the death of a person.

When the guard and I reach the girls' unit, the double doors click open and I step inside. The smell of chlorine fills my nose and I chew hard on my spearmint gum. A wall of windows overlooks a small, concrete courtyard with a single basketball hoop. Across the courtyard, boys wearing orange jumpsuits walk around their unit. There are five girls on the unit; all of them are seated at the table and none are watching the boys. Instead, all of them are silent. Even Missy May, who for the last three weeks has told me how she doesn't have anything to write, has nothing to say to me. Usually the girls are so chatty it takes me half of the hour-long writing workshop to quiet them down to write.

"What's going on?" I pull out a chair, dump my bag on the floor, and sit down next to Missy May. The afternoon snack of oranges and milk sit on the table, unopened and uneaten. No one looks at me.

I look toward Katie, the guard, who sits at the circular desk in the unit. Katie is the one guard whose name I always remember. My first week, Katie made a folder for the poetry workshop and we keep all the poems inside. She often jokes and talks to the girls and is attentive to their needs. But today she stares at her computer and does not look up.

Slowly I open our latest poetry chapbook and find a poem to read. There are often tears accompanying the poetry reading, but today I'm not even two lines into reading when a girl starts crying. The girl is new and I don't recognize her from previous workshop sessions. Before I can do anything, the girl's crying turns into hyperventilating. Frantically, I wave the guard over to the table. Katie gently guides the girl out of the writing circle and calls for the nurse. I take a deep breath and look around the circle. No one meets my eyes.

"Do you want me to read more?" I ask. I'm not sure what to do and no one is giving me any hints as to what might be going on. There can be a lot of things which upset the girls, from court dates that don't go the way they hope to visitors who don't show up to being booked into units with rivals, but today none of this seems to be the case.

I glance at the clock on the concrete wall. I've only been here five minutes. It feels like thirty minutes. I flip to a different page and begin again to read.

I'm barely into the second poem when another girl starts giggling. She was new last week, and I am not sure if her name is Kathleen or Caitlin. "What's so funny?" I ask.

"I'm sorry. I just giggle when I get upset."

Across the table, Tabby and Sherry, two regulars in the workshop, have their hands crossed across their chests.

"Tabby? Sherry? What's going on?"

"Everyone is just pissing me off today." Tabby glares at the table.

"Do we have to write?" Sherry asks.

Usually Sherry enjoys poetry workshop, so I'm surprised by her question. "What's wrong?" I repeat.

"I just don't want to write," Sherry says and shrugs.

"Maybe you will in a little bit." My words fall flat around the circle.

Beside me, Missy May says nothing.

I reach into my bag and pull out *The Book of Qualities*, by J. Ruth Gendler. The book is illustrated emotions brought to life with human qualities in prose poetry. It's a good way to incorporate personification while at the same time being able to discuss that there are more emotions than just angry and sad—the two most common emotions in the poetry workshop.

I can't find an emotion which addresses the girls today and instead end up reading "Confidence."

Confidence ignores "No Trespassing" signs. It is as if he doesn't see them. He is an explorer, committed to following his own direction. He studied mathematics in France and still views his life as a series of experiments. The only limits he respects are his own. He is honest and humble and very funny. After all these years, his sister doesn't understand why he still ice skates with Doubt.

When I finish, I look up. Sherry stares out the large windows of the unit. Across the glass windows, the boys in 2E are getting out their schoolwork from plastic tubs placed next to each cell door. She doesn't seem to see any of them.

"Should I read another one?" I ask. "Do you think this will help you write today?"

"Can we just write whatever we want?" Tabby asks.

"I guess. But I hoped some of you might choose an emotion and personify it. Where does it live? What does it like to eat? Where does it hide? Who does it hide from?" My words sound foolish to me and I can't figure out how to reach the girls where they are.

"Our friend was found on the road," Sherry says suddenly. She doesn't turn to look at me.

"What?" I drop the book of emotions on the table. It lands face-down with the pages bent.

"You knew her," Tabby said. "I think she was in here once for poetry workshop."

"Recently?"

"A couple weeks ago," Sherry says.

Suddenly, I am pulling out the manila folder where I keep all the girls' poems. "What's her name?"

Sherry tells me the girl's name and I am on a frantic hunt to find her poems.

"You can send her dad the poems," Sherry says. "Maybe he can read them at the funeral." Her voice is flat and empty. "She was coming home from a party and got tired of waiting for her dad to pick her up. She walked."

I thumb through the poems as memories of Dad sitting in my

Saturday morning gymnastics classes flash across my mind. Other parents dropped their kids off and the ones who stayed sat in folding chairs along the edges of the gym, intently watching their kids and sometimes calling out commands or directions. Dad brought his Saturday paper, and while I tumbled, flew over the vault, and balanced on the beam, he read. Afterward, he drove a friend and me to the local Hallmark store where I spent my weekly allowance and babysitting money on small blue Smurf figurines. When I started dating, Dad drove me on my dates until I was old enough to drive. It would have never occurred to me to walk home because I never had to worry Dad would not be there waiting for me.

I reach the end of the stack of poetry and come up with nothing. If she wrote a poem, she did not give it to me. "I don't have any of her poems," I say quietly.

Tears slide down Sherry's face. Suddenly, I am furious. Why didn't the guards tell me? Why didn't someone say something to me on the way into the units? Someone could have told me. I could have been prepared. I could have planned something to talk to the girls about grief and loss. But I am not prepared, and our emotional poetry exercise seems pointless in the reality of this moment. I want to do something, but I am as powerless as the girls with my grief.

Suddenly, Missy May pushes a piece of paper to me. "Read it."

I pick up the poem as Missy May leans against my elbow. Her nappy hair brushes against my arm.

I quickly read Missy May's poem. The poem pulls me in as she personifies *powerless* to be a monster.

When I finish, Missy May says, "I've got a few more things to say." She reaches for a stack of notebook paper.

Missy May was the only one who wrote today.

Teen Boy

IF I COULD CHANGE MY LIFE

When I was little, I was a good kid.
I remember playing with other kids
Just to pass the time
And listening to birds chime.

Now I'm seventeen, committing adult crimes
And if I could change my life
I'd go back to being a little kid
When I used to fly kites
And ride bikes
When I was little.

Call It Courage, August 2006.

HIGH SCHOOL CREATIVE WRITING

On a rainy day in April, just after the spring-break holiday, I stand in front of the local high school creative writing class. The creative writing teacher, Jennifer, and I have worked for two years to find funding for a series of creative writing workshops. Jennifer is frustrated the creative writing class has become a dumping ground for kids, and teachers, who think it's an easy elective class. She's hopeful the four-week workshop will give more meaning to the class. I have a hard time believing a workshop taught by a writer who doesn't have a published book with her name on the cover is going to make an impact.

I wait for the bell and shift on my feet in front of the classroom. The kids drift in from the open door and hardly look at me. They are more interested in talking to each other and looking bored. I've worn my black platform shoes which give me a feeling of power, but the sweat still begins to creep down the back of my shirt. A copy of a paperback book, *Summer Shorts*, lies face down on a table beside me. My short story "Hurricanes" is included in the collection. The story is about the summer trip we took with my dad after my parents were divorced. I saw the call for submissions at one of my first Seattle Society of Children's Book Writers and Illustrators meetings. Each month, various opportunities for children's writers scrolled across a large screen from a PowerPoint prepared by the regional advisors.

Miriam Hess at Blooming Tree Press was looking for "summer adventure" stories for age eight to eleven. As a last-semester MFA student, I felt some confidence in my writing abilities. After the meeting, I sat down and wrote a story so close to my real life, I forgot to change the names of the characters to fictional names. I also left my sister out of the story. I tried to explain I only had so many words in a short story, but still, I disappointed her. I had shown her what my parents have said for years—I did not want a sister. My sister is eleven years younger than me and I have tried to tell everyone that it was more a matter of not wanting to know my parents were having sex than not wanting a sister. But no one believes me, and this story was just more proof that I have left her out of the family.

In the high school creative writing class, I stare at the paperback book as if I don't know my own story is inside and I don't have copies of the paperback at home. Jennifer tells me she read it to the kids. I can't imagine high school students who are too interested in a story for ten-year-olds. "Hurricanes" is my first published story, but somehow one story in an anthology doesn't feel like enough to be calling myself a published author. Neither does the small stack of articles I've published in various writers' periodicals. In my mind, the only thing which will define me as a published author is a book contract from a traditional publisher and an agent to broker the deal—something which seems always just out of my grasp.

I step to the overhead projector table where I have set my notes and papers for the workshop. Absently, I shuffle the stack. Still, I'm more uncomfortable standing in front of the creative writing class than I am at the detention center. As a high school sophomore, I wanted nothing more than to be in the creative writing class. Creative writing was taught by the facilitator of the cheer team, and everyone knew that you had a better chance at making the highly competitive squad if you had taken Mrs. Allen's creative writing class. I wanted nothing more than to wear the flared red-and-white skirts. I had watched the team practice in the parking lot across from our house for years. I'd seen the girls get out of their cars on game days, wearing their red-and-white skirts. I'd seen how they always had large groups of friends and lots of boys around them. In my mind, the only way to be successful at high school was to be on that squad.

A freshman couldn't try out for the squad, but at the beginning of sophomore year, the stars aligned and I got into the creative writing class; I knew I had a chance to be on that squad once Mrs. Allen got to know me. I liked making up stories. I'd been making up stories since my parents sat on the floor with me and played Little People with the wooden Fisher-Price people and their little yellow house. In middle school, I had loved my language arts class. We participated in a writer's workshop where we filled manila folders with stories and poems. As a seventh-grade teacher, I taught using the same writing workshop approach. By that point, famed educator Nancie Atwell had evolved the workshop to include much more than just filling a manila folder with creative stories and poems.

But when my sophomore semester creative writing class started, it became very apparent that Mrs. Allen favored the girls who were already on cheer team. These were the same girls I knew from the summer pool. They lay on their thick towels, lathered with baby oil, while I spent days horsing around on the raft with my brother and two friends.

The sophomore creative writing class was unlike my eighth-grade language arts class where we had taken the point of view of objects, and written stories and journal entries about our life. In high school, we read classic short stories, dissected them, and wrote character sketches about real people. And we never wrote anything about our own life.

By the time tryouts rolled around, I hadn't impressed Mrs. Allen in class. She never chose my work to read aloud and she never wrote comments about how much she liked my writing. During tryouts, I did my best, but was cut by the first round. "You just didn't smile enough or seem lively enough," one of the cheer girls told me later. I didn't know how to tell her it was too hard to smile when my parents were getting divorced. By that point, Mom was hauling my brother and me to twelve-step meetings about alcoholism at the local hospital, and I was spending Saturday nights at my Dad's basement apartment eating spaghetti, and trying to pretend everything was okay to everyone around me. I couldn't imagine how I could have smiled in those tryouts.

I push away my high school memories as the bell rings. Jennifer sits at her desk in the back of the room and calls out student names, marking absent kids on a computer-based list that will be sent to the main office. She's almost finished when the classroom door opens. A boy saunters in and slides into the last row of desks. The boy's jeans hang low and he wears a dark sweatshirt. His dark hair is cut in a bowl and his bangs hang in his eyes.

Jennifer doesn't look up from her computer. She doesn't ask the boy for a late pass. She doesn't ask where he's been or why he's late, and not one of the thirty-two students turn to look at him. Jennifer finishes attendance and, without moving from her desk, says, "The writer I told you about is here today."

A few of the kids look at me. But most of them stare downward at their desks or the floor or the clock. My heart races and the sweat now rolls down my back. In the detention center, I have the attention of the kids immediately. They look forward to coming to the workshop and are eager to do something besides sit in their cells. But the school creative writing class is different. I need their attention and, in their eyes, I am not offering them anything interesting.

I pick up one of the Denney poetry books. "I'm going to read you some poetry."

A few of the faces look up at me. Most keep their eyes averted.

"This poem is written by teens at Denney Juvenile Justice Center."

Suddenly, all eyes are on me. Most of the kids know Denney Juvenile Justice Center. It is the only juvenile detention facility for our county. The high school has its fair share of school fights and drug possession, and most have seen a police car parked outside the nearby Target or Safeway, waiting to escort a teen shoplifter into the backseat of the waiting car. I flip open the page and read a poem about a young lady and the abuse she experiences at the hands of her father.

When I look up, most of the kids are watching me. A few squirm in their chairs and avoid my eyes. The honest and real poems have skated the edges of some of their secrets. The secrets are kept close like my own secrets I tucked away in high school. I quickly glance at Jennifer. She looks over her class, checking for their reactions and gauging the mood of the class. Once she determines the class temperature is fine, she nods at me. As much as Jennifer complains about the creative writing class being a dumping ground, she is an excellent teacher. Jennifer was the alternative middle school teacher for years. She is one of those teachers whom kids confide in. She knows how to reach kids where they are and encourages them to succeed.

And suddenly, I know why Jennifer hired me to run the workshops. It doesn't matter that I am not a multi-published author. It doesn't matter that I don't have a large advance for a two-book deal. Jennifer asked me to teach in her class because I am showing the kids how to tap into their own stories, just like I did with "Hurricanes."

"I want to read you another poem," I say. My shoulders relax and I meet the eyes of a handful of kids in the middle of the room. I briefly explain how the next poem was inspired by a poem published in *You Hear Me? Poems and Writing by Teenage Boys,* edited by Betsy Franco. It's a poem about the way a boy's father perceives him and how that perception impacts him. I ask the kids to think about how others perceive them. I encourage them to think about their family, friends, and community. I tell them that how they are seen in the eyes of others will be the topic for writing today.

"Do we have to share these?" someone asks from the left side of the room.

I look to Jennifer for guidelines. In the detention center workshop, I allow the kids the freedom to decide if they will share their poems or not.

I don't grade them on their writing. The workshop is about the process, rather than the product. But the school classroom is different. There are certain things Jennifer must read and grade.

"Write these in your journal," Jennifer says. "You can fold over the edge of the paper if you don't want me to read them."

I smile at Jennifer, grateful to her for showing the kids she trusts them and encouraging them to write from their heart and find their voices through their personal stories. I turn back to the class. The boy who has come in late has his hand in the air. I glance at Jennifer to see if she wants to respond to him. He shakes his head at her and nods to me. "You," he mouths to me.

I walk down the aisle as the kids settle into the poem writing. I can't help but feel a little bit of pride that one of the kids wants to talk to me about his poetry.

"You're the poetry lady who comes to Denney," the boy says in a straightforward voice.

"Do I know you?" I stare hard at him. He doesn't look familiar, but I often don't recognize the kids when they're not in their detention center orange.

"I just got out," he shrugs. "I was there for the last couple days."

"Did you get one of the new poetry books?" They have just been printed. Tomorrow, I will distribute them at the poetry workshop, but I have brought along a few extra to the school workshop. I will leave one with Jennifer and a couple for the school guidance counselors.

"Nah," he says. "I don't want one."

"Okay." I understand. He doesn't want anything which reminds him of the detention center and his time there.

"Remember when we lost that pencil?" the boy says. "Good thing we found that!"

My memory clicks. Alex is the boy who was searched for the missing pencil. He's the one who told me it was no big deal for the mistake I made in counting, causing him to be searched.

"Alex," Jennifer says from her desk. "Do you have your missing work?"

Alex's face closes off. He crosses his arms and leans back in his chair.

Jennifer's question sets off a long and defiant conversation between the two of them until finally, exasperated, she tells him that if he doesn't turn anything in, he won't pass the class. Alex merely shrugs as the classroom phone rings.

With a long sigh, Jennifer picks up the phone. She listens and then replaces the receiver. "Alex, go to the counseling center."

Alex slides out of his chair and saunters to the door slowly. At the door, he turns and nods to me before he struts out of the classroom.

Jennifer shakes her head. "He's been in and out all semester. He probably won't pass. That's probably what they're telling him at the counseling center. They've been calling kids in all day to give them the news."

I'm not sure if Jennifer knows Alex has been in detention, but from her conversation, I guess she does not. The information didn't get passed down the pipeline of endless emails between administrator and teacher. I pick up a piece of paper on Alex's desk. It's a poem about when he was little and how he enjoyed flying kites and listening to birds. He ends by saying he wants to go back to being little. While I was explaining the poetry process to the class, he has written his poem. He doesn't need the explanation. He already knows how to write poetry from the heart. Alex knows the secret I still can't completely grasp, how to write about real experiences and tell the truth.

I hand the poem to Jennifer. She reads it and says, "It's the first thing he's written all semester."

"Do you want to keep the poem?" I ask.

Jennifer nods and slips it into an empty manila folder. "He's got one assignment done."

She smiles at me. "Thank you."

WHEN DARKNESS FELL ON ME

One day, I was me.
The next I wasn't.
That's when darkness fell on me.
It was dark and cold
I was scared,
had to steal to live.
I never knew what it meant to love.

I was always confused
Getting held back in school
Blinded by the darkness
I began to be wild
I called myself a lone wolf
Fierce and dependent on no-one
But myself
Doing what I wanted to do.

I wish I could go back and change
The day that darkness fell on me
Mixed feelings of sadness, fear, loneliness
And feelings I can't share
Because I don't even understand them.

The darkness has trapped me
I can't see.
It's cold and lonely.
Darkness has fallen on me.

Because I Wanted To Be Loved, January 2009.

THE MONSTERS WE FIGHT

Missy May doesn't stay out long once she is released. She's back within a few weeks, and this time, I meet her in the classroom.

"May I see one of my poems?" Missy May stops in front of me as the unit files in around her.

Six girls sit down at the two-person tables in the classroom. Two of the girls talk loudly about their court dates and upcoming sentences. I reposition two girls at different tables while a guard barks at Missy May to sit down.

Missy May continues to stand in front of me. "My poem," she demands.

"Not now," I say sharply. "Sit down." I'm not in the mood to deal with Missy May's demands. This morning, I've received another rejection on my novel. This is the worst I've gotten so far. The manuscript moved to acquisitions—a process in which top editors and marketing people consider if this is a story they can sell to readers. I'd received an email telling me the first editor really liked the story and could see it in their publishing house. The editor was hopeful it would pass through the committee and be accepted. For the last two weeks, I've been checking my email constantly, waiting for the final yes. Finally, it is my turn! I'd composed the email I would send everyone with my good news and now I was just waiting to hit *send*.

But this morning, there is the rejection email. The book has not sold. Again. "It's just too quiet of a story," the response comes back to me. "We're so sorry."

I'm so sorry too, and this time, I'm pretty sure I'm giving up. I can't get up and send the book out again. I can't take anymore. I've revised the story so many times I don't know where to revise it. The agents don't want it and the publishers don't want it. No one wants it and the whole thing is coming too close to reminding me of the echo of high school when I never could get a boyfriend. I'm beginning to think there must be something so very wrong with me and, whatever it is, I just don't see it but everyone else does.

I've spent all morning on email with a writing friend from graduate school. She is trying to talk me out of jumping off the cliff, but it's not working. It doesn't matter that by this point, I've published everything from articles to short stories. I still can't seem to land that elusive book contract. I'm giving up writing and burning the manuscript.

"Can I have my poem?" Missy May's voice rises clearly from her spot in the middle of the room.

I meet her eyes and am jarred back to the moment. I'm here to teach poetry workshop, not have a pity party about my own writing. I grab the manila folder filled with the girls' poems. It's late March and the folder is thick with poems waiting to be typed for the annual poetry book. I find Missy May's poem lodged in the middle of the stack. "Sorry," I say as I walk over and lay the poem on Missy May's desk. "Here is your poem." I give her an apologetic smile, hoping she'll forgive me for my lack of attention and self-absorbed thoughts instead of paying attention to her.

Missy May reads the poem. Without asking, she slowly gets out of her chair. She walks across the room to the trash can. In one swoop, she crumbles the poem and tosses it into the trash.

"Why did you do that?" I gasp.

Outside the windows of the classroom, a guard moves toward the door. I shake my head and motion him away. I am able to handle Missy May.

"It's not good," Missy May says. "I don't want you to publish it."

"I think you should sit down," I say quietly. I nod my head, just briefly, toward the guard still standing outside the door. Missy May doesn't bother to look at the guard. She walks back to her seat, not looking at me.

The six other girls in the room watch me. I look away and to the concrete walls which have colorful drawings hanging on them. At the top of each drawing is one word. "IF." The drawings are a part of The IF Project which has recently visited Denney. The IF Project began at the Washington Correction Center for Women when Seattle Police Department Detective Kim Bogucki asked a group of prisoners: *If there was something someone could have said or done that would have changed the path that led you here, what would it have been?* Detective Bogucki's question inspired inmate Renata Abramson, who shared this question and collected answers from her fellow prisoners. Now, formerly incarcerated speakers lead discussions with youth on why people have made the choices they have. When I see The IF Project panel of speakers at Denney, it is a powerful presentation of personal experience with incarceration as well as discussion on how each person answers the IF question.

I wonder how Missy May would answer that IF question. How would I?

"What are we writing?" Caitlin asks. She leans forward on her desk, and reminds me there are six other girls waiting for me to begin our session.

"Sorry," I shake my head as I apologize for the second time in five minutes. "I'm a little distracted today." I don't share about my submission process. Sometimes the teens ask me about how much money a writer makes, and I always tell them honestly, don't quit the day job. In my school visits, I talk to kids about the process of submission and how much patience and persistence is needed. I don't share this with the teens in detention because, in my eyes, until I have that first book contract, I am not really a writer. And if I am not really a writer, then why am I pretending to be one with them? I know the kids and their honesty. I fear they will call me on this imposter game and I will have to leave the poetry workshop, and right now the poetry workshop is the only thing in my writing life which continues to make sense to me. The weekly time I spend teaching the workshop is the only time I feel like some part of me remembers why I wanted to be a writer.

I dig into my bag and pull out white sheets of paper and a copy of *Where the Wild Things Are*, by Maurice Sendak. Suddenly there is a chorus of voices. "We love that book!"

I smile the first real smile since I've received the rejection. "We're going to talk about monsters," I say. "While I'm reading, I want you to think about monsters in your life. Think about those monsters who you fight all the time. The monster could be a drug addiction. It could be a message you tell yourself about not being good enough, pretty enough, or smart enough."

I lean back against the desk and begin to read the familiar words written by Sendak. In front of me, the girls are quiet, listening to every word. I suspect most of them have not had very many experiences with adults reading them picture books. I make a mental note to read more picture books to them and give them the experience, if just for a few minutes, of having someone read a story to them. When I am finished, I hand out colored-pencil packs to each table. The teacher whose room I'm using always has colored pencils available, and unlike the number-two writing pencils, we don't have to keep the colored pencils in Styrofoam spheres. "How about we draw a monster and write about 'the monster in me'? Let's have a conversation with that monster. See what it wants to say to you, and then write that down."

The girls lean over and begin to write. I glance at Missy May. She draws on her paper and doesn't look at me. Quietly, I go to the trash can and pick up her poem. I unfold it, and place the paper back inside the manila folder. I don't say anything to Missy May and she doesn't say anything else to me the rest of the workshop. When it comes time to turn in poetry and drawings, Missy May slips her drawing into her manila folder, and following her unit, shuffles out the door.

The following week, Missy May enters the classroom and is bright and talking constantly. She asks about her poem and says she wants to see it. I show her the same poem she tossed away. Missy May reads through it and smiles. She waves it in the air and tells everyone she's got a poem that might be in the book. Missy May tells me to keep it and requests a release form. She doesn't mention having thrown the poem away, and I don't remind her. When I talk to Eric on the way out of the units about Missy May, he tells me it's the drugs and the coming off of them in detention that makes her mood swings. He thanks me for continuing to believe in her, and in his words I hear the echo to my own writing rejection. No matter the amount of rejections on my novel, now titled *Stained Glass Summer*, I will keep believing in the story I am telling until it finds a path to publication.

A year later, after receiving the release form, I publish the poem Missy May threw away in our yearly book. She is back in detention when I hand our books out, and proudly reads her poem to the unit. She never mentions throwing it away, and I don't either. I'm not sure if she forgot, if the drug use affected her memory or if she simply doesn't want to remember, but I follow her lead and I don't mention that day her poem ended up in the trash either.

During that same year, *Stained Glass Summer* would be published. Tired of hitting dead ends with traditional publishing, I took a risk on the tide of a new influx of e-book publishers. The digital-first publishers have been in the romance markets for the last few years. I heard about them while attending Seattle Romance Writers Association Conferences, but they're new to the children's markets. Once accepted for publication, my book is assigned an editor, cover artist, and marketing support. I am paid royalties and do not pay for my book to be published. I'm not a hundred-percent sure that what I've done isn't suicide for both my career and the novel, but I couldn't keep going down the same road. In the teen writing workshops I facilitate at libraries and schools, I see the readers for this story and I want them to have it. And, just like Missy May's poem, no one would ever read it if I gave up and left it in the "trash" of my computer files.

I remember that sunny day in early August when I sat in a neighborhood coffee shop and pressed the *send* button on my email to Celina Sumers at Musa Publishing. Within a week, Celina has requested the story, and it sells. *Stained Glass Summer* pops up on Amazon, timed to hit after the holidays when people are anxious to fill new e-readers and gadgets. The sales numbers creep upwards and I have become a published author.

I will see Missy May one more time in poetry workshop. Her orange T-shirt and baggy pants stretch over her bulging thighs and middle. Her eyes are dull and empty as she tells me she has a daughter, but doesn't have her in full-time custody. Missy May talks as though it's someone else's child and not hers who is living with her aunt. Missy May asks me for paper and tells me she has a lot of poetry to write. As she works, I study her and search for the girl I once sent to her cell. I search for the girl who leaned against me like a dog who needed to be petted. I see nothing of that girl in the Missy May who sits in front of me. In one of our regular conversations, Eric tells me it's the drugs she has been using for too long. Crack. Heroine. The hard drugs. But are drugs the only things that have dulled her?

Throughout the workshop, as I am helping the other girls, I listen for Missy May's voice. I want her to call to me for help. I want to hear her chattering about her sentences, the damn judge, and everything else that is unfair in her life. I want to hear her boasting about the poetry she's had published in our annual books. But I hear nothing.

I hand out *Stained Glass Summer* bookmarks to the girls and tell them how, the night before, I found pieces of broken glass shards on the floor of the hot-glass shop at the local art center during a workshop with the teens who are participating in the new Promising Artists in Recovery Program. The scattered pieces of fragmented glass are the same kind of glass a friend once gave to me, ten years ago, which sparked the idea for *Stained Glass Summer.* I keep glancing at Missy May out of the corner of my eye, hopeful my story will spark an interest in her. She never looks up from her writing.

The girls ask me if I'll ever write about them. I tell them maybe one day I will write about the poetry workshop. Maybe, I say, if I have the courage, like you, to write about my life, I will write about our workshop. And I hope that someday, I do have the courage like the kids in orange to write about my own life. I hope I can tell my story as truthfully as they tell their story.

At the end of the hour, Missy May is still writing. I ask her if she'd like to read her poems aloud and she declines. "You keep them," she pushes them toward the end of her desk, "for that book." Her words sound as if she can't even remember the names of our books, the ones she has been published in and once waved around the room so proudly.

As I lean over to pick up a poem, Missy May's voice speaks softly. "I wrote them for my daughter."

Without reading the papers, I push them back to Missy May. "You should keep these," I say. "Give them to your daughter." I do not want to hold onto Missy May's poems and run the risk we won't get release forms. The poems will be tossed to the bottom of the manila folder and, this time, it's important the poems stay with Missy May and her daughter.

Missy May doesn't argue with me. She slips the poems inside her manila folder. "You won't see me anymore," she says. "I'm eighteen in another two weeks. I'm moving over to the county jail."

I want to reach over and hug Missy May. I want to take the darkness that engulfs her and remove it for good so she can walk out of the detention center and start a new life with her daughter. I want tell her to take care of herself. I want to tell her things will work out, but I don't know if they will. I don't know if they *can* work out. And as I watch her walk out the door for the last time, hands grasped behind her, leading the other girls back to the unit, I see the big gang girl who didn't write poetry, and I softly say goodbye to her in the empty classroom.

REMEMBERED

When I die, how will people think of me with the life I lead now? Will they think I was smart or stupid for all the things I did? Will they think I was kind or mean for getting into fights? Will they think I was funny or were they just laughing at me for being dumb? Will I be missed or will I be forgotten? How will I be remembered?

Call It Courage, August 2006.

TOO MANY FACES IN THE NEWSPAPER

It seems that every spring a kid in orange shows up on the front page of the newspaper. When I run the poetry workshop in the units, I never know what crimes the kids commit. Later when I move the workshop to the school day and am required to take attendance, sometimes I will see small codes and abbreviated letters of a crime type beside a child's name. I always quickly look away. In the workshop, they are not allowed to discuss anything related to why they are in detention. I like this rule. It allows me to meet the teen as a writer. Sometimes, when I sit at my kitchen table and open the paper to see another headline with a familiar face staring back at me, I consider canceling my subscription. But I am the daughter of two journalists, and subscribing to the paper is the same as paying the monthly electric bill. It's not something to be canceled.

I don't watch the news very often, preferring to spend my evenings on the computer or reading, but on a rainy evening, I flip on the TV while I cook dinner. Half-hearted, I listen to a report about a young man who has died of a drug overdose. I hear this same story the next day on my car radio. There is mention of a girlfriend and a daughter, but no name is released.

By the time I open my Wednesday paper, the boy's name and photo are released.

Josh Wiggs.

I sink onto my green couch and stare at the picture and try to focus. It can't be Josh. Not Josh who was in trouble with Anne Marie. Not Josh who works so hard on his poems—the same poems I have set aside to be included in our next book.

My eyes blur and I can barely read the crisp black print which tells me Josh's funeral is today.

It takes all my strength to walk upstairs to my loft office. I stumble past the dog, who lies by my desk. At thirteen, she sleeps more than she is awake. I am waiting fearfully for that moment when I'll have to take the final drive to the vet's office and let her go, knowing that the heaviness which threatens to pull me under now will again drag me into the dark. I pull out the folder where I keep the poems. Josh's are near the top because I saw him a few weeks ago. His poems are heartfelt, about his girlfriend, daughter, and mom. It's the second time Josh's poems would have been included in our yearly book.

I swallow like I have rocks in my throat, and my stomach tightens but I can't cry. I feel as if I am moving through a play where I am watching myself, unable to connect to the loss in this moment. Josh was in detention on the day I handed out our last book of poetry. I asked him to read his poem. When Josh finished, the twelve boys on the unit applauded. Josh fiddled with his pencil and said quietly, "You know. I didn't used to like poetry." He stared intently at me. "Poetry is a way to express yourself. You can really tell people how you feel."

I hear Josh's voice as he tells me, in Anne Marie's class, that poetry is important.

"Yes, Josh," I say quietly as I sit down at my desk, "I hear you."

Quickly, I email Eric and request Josh's home address. I'm not sure what the rules are for releasing the kid's address and home information, but I'm hoping in this one case, they'll make an exception.

While I wait for Eric's response, I write a letter to Josh's mom. I tell her how much Josh meant to the poetry workshop. I tell her how much we enjoyed his poetry, and I enclose all of the poems I have held for the next poetry book. I place the one he wrote to her on the top.

I look at the clock. I really want to go to the funeral. But the funeral is at the same time as the poetry workshop. How can I skip the poetry workshop? One boy is dead, but twelve boys are still living, and they are waiting for this workshop.

At the detention center, Eric meets me on the other side of the double doors. His face is closed and his usual smile and joking are absent. He hands me a small piece of paper with Josh's address. I stick the paper in my bag and walk beside him. Neither of us talks as we climb up the stairwell to the classrooms. The only sound is our hard-soled shoes as they click on the linoleum floor.

When we reach the classroom, Eric walks to the desk and picks up the roster. "I thought these boys would be best today."

I take the stapled paper and read through the familiar names of Josh's unit. I read the names and some part of me registers Josh's name should be on this list. Josh should be coming through the door, with his curly blond hair bobbing on his head. Josh should be saying, "I've got a new poem today." But instead, Josh's name is not there, and a part of me still can't connect this is real. I can't connect what is happening in the newspaper to the blond boy who I talked to just last week about his poetry. How can that boy be gone? How can that boy be dead? How can the boy I knew have died of a drug overdose when the last conversation I had with him was about his pride in staying sober?

The other names from Josh's unit are the boys who come back the most and are serving time for drug-related crimes. The majority of these boys are in drug court, which requires the kids to attend Alcoholics Anonymous or Narcotics Anonymous, go to school, do community service, and complete regular check-in with court-appointed drug classes and regular urine analysis (UA). It is a UAs that most often cause the boys to circle back through the detention center, when they show a teen has used again, if only briefly. Most of the time, their return stay is brief. These boys are some of my favorites at the detention center. They remind me of my brother and a boy I once dated who was in recovery.

I lay out the books in the poetry workshop and I don't have to think about a topic. Our topic today is loss. The plastic sandals clop on the floor as the boys file into the room. There is no joking. No laughing. There is barely any talking. The boys slip into seats and slump. I glance at the clock. 1:45 p.m. Josh's funeral starts in fifteen minutes.

"We're going to write about loss," I say. My voice sounds heavy and I'm glad today the boys don't need a lot of instruction. I'm not sure I can speak much.

I hand out paper and wait to see what they need today. I am relieved the boys don't need me to read poems to them. They don't need to have discussion. The boys don't need me to clarify loss. Instead, all eight boys write. The room is silent except for the scratch of pencils.

And today I also pull out a piece of paper and write. I write about Josh and how it felt to have him as a writer in the poetry workshop and how it feels now that he's gone. The minutes fly, and when I look up again, it is time to share the poems. Again, there is no bravado before sharing, no chatter. Instead, the boys read. They read poems of loss of family, loss of girlfriends, and loss of trust after relapses.

As they read, I feel Josh in the workshop. He is here with us. He is listening to us read poems and he is telling us, *poetry is important.* I will feel this same sense of presence when my father dies. The last morning Dad is alive, I will feel him as I move through my weekly yoga class. As I shift through sun salutation and downward dog, memories will flash across my mind. Memories I have long forgotten and I won't remember in such detail and color after that morning is over. But, in that one hour in yoga, a brightly colored movie will upload into my mind. I am five. I am six. I am seven. I am at the park with Dad. I am at the Illinois State Fair. I am riding bikes to the campus of University of Illinois. We are eating popcorn while we play games and we are planting a garden. Later I will learn Dad was in surgery during that hour of yoga. He will not make it out of that surgery. And I will believe that a part of me, a part of my childhood, was in that moment with Dad as he was leaving.

After the workshop, I drive the car across the street to a little park. It's a sunny spring afternoon, and thick, puffy clouds move slowly above my head. Ever since I started at the detention center, I have always brought the dog with me. She sleeps in the backseat, and afterward we take walks at the park. It helps to have Nadia greet me, as seeing the soft, warm, blond wiggling dog eases some of the sadness I feel each week from the workshop.

Even though Nadia struggles to run due to a heart condition which will take her life, she still has the enthusiasm of a young dog as soon as she sees her park. I clip her leash on, open the door, and lift her to the ground; she's long past the age of being able to jump in and out of the car by herself. Nadia sniffs at trash cans. I take long, deep breaths, breathing in the clean, fresh air full of springtime hope. The pink cherry trees are in bloom, and a few yellow daffodils bob in the light breeze in front yards. I give Nadia's leash a yank away from the trash can, and we wander down the blacktop pavement toward the swings. A small boy pumps higher and higher. He calls out to his Grandma, "Watch me!"

The boy flies higher and higher. His joyful, young voice soars over the concrete building of the detention center looming behind him. This young boy jumps out of the swing and flies through the air, landing in the sand in a giggling heap. As his Grandma holds out her hand to help him stand, I think about the boy named Josh who once wrote poetry, and how once, not too long ago, all of the boys in that concrete building behind me were young and flying through the air, calling for someone to watch them, too.

DAD

"Your dad," my aunt's voice cracks on the phone message, "he's in ICU."

I listen to the phone message with a certainty this is the moment. Earlier in the year, I had a premonition about Dad. My aunt had called too early on a fall morning. "Sorry," she told me, "I forgot about the time zone." That morning, I waited for her to tell me something was wrong with Dad. But she didn't. Not that morning.

But now, she is telling me something is wrong. Dad is in ICU and this is the moment which I have danced around, skated around, and edged around all my life. It is here, and there will be no dancing, skating, or avoiding. I am the twelve-year-old girl sitting on the edge of my parents' bed as Dad tells me he is moving out of the house, but this time there will be no future visitations.

Dad has been sick for the last month. Days after his seventieth birthday, my brother and sister started asking me, "Have you heard from Dad? Dad hasn't been on Facebook." Dad loved Facebook and we begin to worry when days pass without a status update from him commenting on his neighbors, the lady he's still in love with, or something he's just barbequed.

A few days later, my brother tells me, "I just talked to Dad. He doesn't sound so good. He says he can't get out of bed. His legs won't work."

Panicked, I call Dad. His voice is weak and groggy, but he answers his cell phone. "I'm fine," he says. "I'll go to the hospital tomorrow." He tells me how he's all set up. He has his cell phone. He has people coming over to check on him. He's fine. His voice sounds the way it did when, as children, my brother and I bothered him too much in the morning and he wanted to be left alone with his paper, pipe, and Bloody Mary. But I am not a child, and I won't let his cranky voice detour me. I am good at persistence and I keep calling.

Dad's excuses in refusing to seek medical help last for a week. He can't find his medical card. He can't find his wallet. He has to get some papers together. He is going to be able to get out of bed tomorrow. At one point I have the luck of calling when my aunt is checking on him. We talk in hushed voices about how to get him to the hospital. She tells me we need his consent. The ambulance can't take him away without his agreement. From his bedroom, I hear Dad yelling, "I hear you talking about me!" Dad's body is giving out, but his spirit is still strong.

By midweek, Dad's condition has deteriorated. He still answers the phone when I call and tells me he'll call for an ambulance tomorrow. But his voice is hoarse and raspy. My aunt visits again. She tells me he hasn't gotten out of bed to change his clothes or go to the bathroom. After I talk to Dad each day, I spend hours lying on my bed, on my back, staring at the ceiling. It's as if my world is tilting, and the only way I can hold my center is to lie down.

On Wednesday night, my aunt calls the medics for him. She says he'll have to refuse them if he really doesn't want to go. He does and, nine hundred miles away, I am petrified. Dad is lying in bed, dying, and he is refusing help. I cannot stop shaking and finally get into bed in the middle of the morning. I pull the covers over me and shake until I drift off into a fitful nap.

The next day, my aunt calls. The relief is evident in her voice. "Your dad called for the ambulance last night," she tells me. "He's at the hospital. I haven't talked to the doctors yet." I lean against the counter in relief. Now someone can find out what's wrong.

The doctor tells my aunt, "Your brother has a drinking problem."

When my aunt calls to tell us, my brother says in a calm, clear, and solid voice, "Dad has had a drinking problem for decades." My brother's line becomes our favorite thing to say for the next few weeks. Everything is "decades."

After a week's stay at the hospital, where Dad is stabilized through vitamins and IVs, he is moved to an assisted rehab. There is no physical diagnosis for why his legs have stopped working beyond that he drinks too much. There is no diagnosis for why he doesn't eat. I spend hours on WebMD. My brother joins me by phone. "Did you check liver failure?" he asks. "How about kidney disease?"

"I'm sure it's reversible," I say. "They can do something about it." Hope falls flat around me like too much rain that can't find a place to pool and ends up causing a hillside to collapse. The end is near, and I know it, but don't want to know it.

When I call Dad in rehab, his voice is slurred and it's hard to understand him. He tells me, "This is really different, Mindy. I don't know…" His voice trails off.

"Just rest, Dad," I say, trying not to think about the last weeks of my grandfather's life last summer. We called him on my birthday in his hospital room where he had been for two months. I couldn't understand his garbled voice any better than I understand Dad's voice now.

I google the symptoms of the dying, looking over my shoulder as if someone is suddenly going to tell me, *You're jinxing things! Your dad is not dying.* I know differently. Dad's symptoms read like a checklist, and the only thing that gives me hope is that he isn't losing interest in his friends or family. He is always glad to see anyone who drops by, and keeps his cell phone by him in the hospital and rehab. If the hospital had a computer, I'm pretty sure he would be posting on Facebook. *He can't be dying,* I tell myself. *Look how interested he is in everyone around him. These are not the signs of someone dying!*

Dad is in rehab for two weeks and I am told they are working on his legs. "But do they know what the problem is?" I ask my aunt. No one answers me, and although I am told a handful of times someone will call me, no one does, and I can't seem to get a number for anyone at the rehab place I can talk to.

There are Facebook updates from his former work friends as they visit. Someone posts Dad's picture on his page. Dad lies on his back in a hospital gown. His face is pale and he's unshaven. "Dad looks kinda bad," my sister and I say to each other.

My sister talks to Dad daily while he is in the rehab. "He sounds kinda lonely," she says.

"Should we go to him?" I ask my brother.

"Dad says no," my brother tells me. "Dad does not want us to see him in the rehab center."

"But when he gets out of the rehab? I can spend some time with him."

"Sure," my brother says. "I think that'd be fine. Dad would like that."

I look up flights and rental cars for late June. My aunt tells me my dad's apartment is small. I look up hotels and the costs begin adding up. Maybe I'll wait, I say, not really sure what I'm waiting for, but something doesn't feel right. I'll make the reservations after Memorial Day weekend, I tell myself.

I call Dad again and try to gauge how he is from nine hundred miles away.

"I'm so tired," Dad says. It's something he's been telling us for weeks. He can't stay awake. No one seems to address that either. But I know it's one of the symptoms of dying. I've read them over and over—wanting and willing for this one to not be there. *Dying is for older people,* I tell myself. *Grandpa was ninety-three when he died. Both of my grandmothers are still living into their nineties. In our family genes, Dad is not old. He just turned seventy. He has decades left.*

"Go to sleep, Dad," I say. "It's okay." It's not okay, nothing is okay, but I don't know what else to say.

Over Memorial Day weekend, I receive emails from Dad's friends: *He doesn't look so good. We have to wear scrubs when we go in. They think he has the flu. He has bad diarrhea.* In my mind, I check off diarrhea on the symptoms of dying. Dad's body is shutting down.

On Memorial Day, I call Dad's cell. He does not answer, and I leave a message. "Happy Memorial Day, Dad." My voice sounds hollow and sad. It is the last message I will leave for Dad.

Then it is Tuesday morning and Dad is in ICU. I pick up the phone and call my aunt's number—a number which I have learned by heart in the last month since Dad became sick.

"The doctors need to talk to you," my aunt says as soon as she answers the phone. "Your dad is not conscious. They found him on the floor of the rehab center this morning. He doesn't have a medical power of attorney. You are the one who must decide."

I swallow hard. I have become my Dad's voice by default of being the oldest child. Dad has been organized all my life—always keeping carefully labeled manila folders for everything. But he has no living will and he has no medical power of attorney. Somehow, Dad has forgotten this final step of organization.

For the next two days, I make the decisions. Each step of the process, I call my brother and sister. "What do you think?" I say. "Breathing tube? CPR? Surgery?" I never knew there were so many decisions to make in one's final hours. Decisions for which we try to guess what Dad would have wanted.

It's this last decision of whether to have surgery or not which stops all of us. Life slows down to a climax moment in a movie. "The surgery can kill him," I tell my siblings. "But he's going to die without the surgery. They think it's the colon that's causing the infection."

"Surgery," my brother says firmly.

"Surgery," I tell the doctor.

Across the country, on a cool, sunny, late May morning, I go off to yoga and Dad goes off to surgery. I am hopeful. The colon will be removed. The infection will be stopped. Dad will be fine. This time, I will make the reservations to see him later this summer. I move through downward dog, sun salutation, and bridge pose, and the memories surround me. I am warm with memories. Memories I have not thought of for decades. I am five. I am seven. I am planting a garden with Dad. We are growing lettuce and cucumbers. I am riding bikes with Dad down a trail to a university student cafeteria which serves chocolate milk. I am in the park across the street with Dad as hot-air balloons land with a whoosh. Dad is here with me; in every pose in yoga, Dad is in the life force with me.

An hour later, I am home from yoga and my aunt calls. "It wasn't the colon," my aunt says. "The doctors need to talk to you."

I hang up and the phone rings immediately. *Norfolk General*, my caller ID says.

"Your dad is not responding," the doctor tells me. His voice is quiet and sad. "I'm sorry."

"Should we come?" I ask. I can barely breathe, but something holds me steady. I have always been good in a crisis and this is no different. I sit down on a kitchen counter stool and place my elbows on the counter. I stare at the window, vaguely aware that it is sunny and the birds are chirping. It is an ordinary May morning and the rest of the world goes to work, attends school, and moves on around me.

"No," the doctor says. "You won't make it in time. Your dad is not responding. He came in to ICU in a coma. He has not responded coming out of surgery. There are things we can do. By the time you get here... But we do need to know…"

"It's okay," I say, "do what you can to make him comfortable." Tears are pouring down my cheeks. "Thank you for trying and keeping me informed." I remember Mom during the days of my grandfather's final hours. My grandfather was a doctor at the hospital where he died, and my mom never forgot her role as his oldest daughter in a small Midwest town. She thanked the hospital staff, coordinated with the funeral home, and sent thank-you cards. I mirror my mother. I have always had good manners in a crisis.

"The chaplain is here," the doctor tells me. "He's with your aunt and father."

"That's nice," I say. I smile through the tears and imagine the chaplain sitting by Dad's bed. I think of Dad in The Church of the Old Donut Shop. I see him reading the Sunday paper and eating his chocolate ring donut. Dad does not need the hospital chaplain at his bedside. It is those of us still living who need the chaplain's comfort. In minutes, my own minister will call me. I've been serving on the church board, and in a quick flurry of high-tech communication from those who surround me during this time, she knows that I need her, not because I am worried about Dad or his soul, but because I am still here, I am still living, and I need her strength as I walk through the goodbye moment.

I hang up the phone with the doctor. I grip the counter with both my hands until my knuckles turn white and I am howling. I am howling in a way I have never cried before; all the tears I have kept inside for the last thirty years every time I have to say goodbye to Dad are erupting. There is something being ripped out of me and it is so excruciating, I cannot breath.

Dad is gone.

CHUCK'S CHILI

Email from Mom. June 3

"Thought you might like this recipe, which I use all the time. It was published in a Panhellenic cookbook while we lived in Wichita, Kansas.—Mom"

2 tbsp cooking oil (I use olive oil)
1 lb hamb
1 tsp salt
2-3 tbsp chili powder
2 small onions, chopped
1 can tomato sauce
1 can tomatoes
1 No. 2 can kidney beans
2 tbsp vinegar

Heat oil, add meat, stir until brown. Add rest of ingredients. Mix well and cover. Simmer 45 minutes, stirring constantly. (Note the "special ingredient" is the vinegar. I often add diced spiced tomatoes instead of whole tomatoes, and various kinds of beans, i.e. chili beans or black beans. Great recipe!)

Chuck Hardwick

COOKING DAD'S DINNER

On the afternoon Dad dies, Mom calls and says she will cook dinner for my sister and me. She says my stepdad is out of town, and it will just be the three of us. Mom says she'll cook Dad's chili and chocolate-chip cookies. I drive two hours to Mom's house, and when I walk in the kitchen, I see a plate of vanilla cupcakes on the table. "What happened to the chocolate-chip cookies?" I ask. "Oh," Mom says. "I guess I wanted cupcakes. Your dad liked chocolate, but I always liked vanilla."

I'm not sure if I'll be able to eat. I haven't eaten anything since I got off the phone with the doctor earlier this morning. But the smell of the chili overpowers my stomach and I take a bite. "This is Dad's chili?" I say through my full mouth. "This is the chili you cook all the time."

Mom smiles and says, "I like your dad's recipes."

For two weeks, I am only able to eat the foods Dad loved: chocolate donuts, shredded cream of wheat smothered in water and doused with butter, and oatmeal. I cook my own pot of chili and I make a big batch of Dad's spaghetti sauce, which I eat for days. While Dad was sick, I ordered him a large box of black popcorn from Amazon. It's the first thing my aunt sends back to me. I open the box and pick up the plastic tub. I can feel the imprint of Dad's fingers still on the plastic container. As the June summer Pacific Northwest sunlight stretches long into ten o'clock, I sit on the couch, eating handfuls of black popcorn out of the same wooden bowls from my childhood, which I practically never use.

My aunt and I have numerous back-and-forth emails about Dad's ashes, what to do with them, where to store them, and who wants to keep them. There are no final instructions from Dad, and we've never talked about it. My brother wants a fancy urn and argues with us about where we will distribute the ashes. My sister and I buy a brick paver for the elementary-school playground where Dad was once Mr. Mom for her kindergarten class. We have his name engraved along with the words *Mr. Mom*. We both know Dad would have loved it.

Can you write your dad's obituary? My aunt asks. *I've tried and I just can't do it. I'm sorry to ask you, but you are a writer, and…* She breaks off in the email.

A small memorial is being planned by some of Dad's work friends. They want to have it at the writing center where he took the memoir classes that my sister and I bought for him over the last two years of birthdays and Father's Days. Across the country, I am not really a part of that planning for Dad's end-of-life celebration, so I am glad to have something to do. I can't seem to absorb that Dad is gone, something which will take me a better part of a year to accept, and even then, on Sunday afternoons, there is an empty feeling which rattles around inside of me. How can it be that I can't pick up the phone and Dad will answer and tell me about the paper he's reading while he sips on his Bloody Mary and dinner cooks in the Crock-Pot? The phone call I've dreaded for over ten years has finally come, and there is a large part of me that doesn't know how to fill the empty space that final phone call leaves. For so long, I have carried a weight inside me. A weight of worry about Dad's health and Dad's drinking. A therapist I saw in my early twenties called it survivor's guilt. She said I feel guilty because my life is good and Dad's is not. She told me this guilt blocks me from having success in my life and I self-sabotage anytime I get close to obtaining success. Almost twenty years after that therapy session, I still didn't realize I carried this weight, until it is gone. Now there is a huge void inside of me—a void which gives me a lot of energy—and I try it to fill by painting the guestroom, trimming every bush and tree in my yard, and furnishing a summer cottage, and yet, I am still rattling around inside.

I talk to my aunt and take notes about Dad's early life for his obituary. Childhood schools, full names of family members, places he lived. I write it all down as if I am preparing for a nonfiction article. For the first time in two weeks, my head clears and the fuzzy feeling lifts as I take notes based on the stories my aunt tells—stories about living in Japan, stories about Dad climbing Mt. Fuji, and stories about Dad's birth in Washington D.C.

After I am finished talking to my aunt, I call Mom. "Can you help with the obituary?" I ask. "Where did Dad work? What were the years? Did he win awards in his writing?"

Together, Mom and I fill in Dad's twenty-year career history as a journalist. Hearst Scholarship Winner at the University of Missouri, farm-beat reporter for the *Champaign Courier*, agriculture writer for the University of Illinois, public relations for Soybean Association, public relations for Ralston Purina, and business owner of the Word Smith—his own independent company. The Dad of my childhood moves across the page of my computer screen and I remember going to visit him in his writing office in an old house in downtown Kirkwood. I sailed through the door, my car keys in my hand, and plunked down in a chair across from his desk. Dad eyed me over his reading glasses, his notes and papers spread across his desk as he worked on writing a brochure or pamphlet. He shared what he was working on, and I'd talk about my day at school. I felt so grown-up in those visits to my writer dad, the visits which were not mandated by my parents' divorce parenting plan but created by my own desire to see Dad. When I work in my writing office, sometimes I can almost see Dad, smiling at me over his spectacles as he takes another puff on his pipe and the smoke drifts around us.

When I am finished writing Dad's obituary, I send it to my brother. "How about Dad's resilient spirit?" my brother says. "What about that?"

I add in, *Dad's resilient spirit will be missed by all.* I edit the obituary one more time, and then email it to the funeral home, who promises to place it for us in the Sunday paper of both Norfolk and St. Louis. I assume it might be a few hundred dollars and my siblings and I will split the cost.

The bill comes back. It's $1010 for the *St. Louis Post-Dispatch.*

My aunt has paid to run the obituary in the Norfolk paper, but she's cut a few lines to help with the cost. I reread the obituary, looking for places where I can cut words. But there is nothing. All of it seems important to Dad's life in St. Louis.

"Run it," my brother says. It's the same tone I heard him say when, as next of kin, we had to approve the final surgery. "Run it."

My brother, sister, and I split the bill, and Dad's obituary is printed in the Sunday *St. Louis Post-Dispatch*, the same paper Dad read religiously with his Bloody Mary and pipe, the paper spread out on the floor, and me standing in the doorway, stuffing my face with a chocolate cream-filled donut from The Church of The Old Donut Shop.

A few days later, my brother tells me how all his friends called or emailed. "They said it was one of the longest ones in the paper!" he tells me.

"Dad would be proud," I say.

I am proud.

My aunt tells us she's cleaning out Dad's apartment. "Is there anything you want?"

"His writing," I say. "And the annual datebooks he kept."

"He has a lot of writing. It's in folders everywhere. He's got drafts and handwritten notes and typed notes, all in the folders."

"Send it all," I say. I know what is inside those folders: Dad's drafts, his notes, and his finished copies. We've talked about it. At one point, a year or so before he died, as he was working on his memoir, Dad told me, "I pulled out all my writing from the storage in the apartment. I don't know what I'm going to do with all of this. You'll have fun sorting through it." He chuckled in that soft laugh I've known all my life, as if death were years away instead of a few months.

"You want the datebooks, too?" my aunt says. "He didn't really write in them. He kept every card sent to him. I can just send the cards to you."

"No," I insist. "Send the datebooks." The datebooks are something my mom's dad, my Grandpa, sent to both my dad and me for years as holiday gifts. Long after my parents divorced, Grandpa continued to send the datebooks to Dad. He dies nine months before Dad, and I inherited his datebooks. I enjoy reading through the dates and years of my childhood. I have tucked Grandpa's yearbooks, labeled and organized, inside plastic boxes in my garage. By the end of the summer, I will add Dad's boxes next to Grandpa's.

"This is going to be expensive for mailing," my aunt says.

"I will send a check, and then send it all media rate. It's all books and papers. It doesn't matter how long it takes for it to get to me." I have gone from being unable to hit the *buy* button on that plane ticket a few weeks ago to writing checks every time I turn around. I don't care. Nothing matters except these few small things that belonged to Dad.

The grief books and bi-weekly counseling sessions I attend at a local hospital tell me the holidays will be hard. But the first one, Father's Day, seems to pass in a haze. It's been less than thirty days since Dad died, and I feel like I don't know what time of year it is, how I should be feeling, or what I should be doing. My sister and I go to an annual sandcastle contest and festival. As we walk up and down the beach, looking at the creations coming to life which in a few hours will be washed out to sea, everything feels like I'm watching it from a distance. Due to a move out of St. Louis and to New York State when Mom remarried, my sister and I haven't spent

Father's Day with Dad since I was in college. Today doesn't really feel that different beyond that there is no phone call to make at the end of the day, something which actually relieves me more than saddens me, as I am not watching the clock and trying to judge when to call him with the three-hour time difference when he will not have had too much time for his nightly Scotch, his words slurred and repetitive.

A few days after Father's Day, I arrive home after running errands. On my doorstep are four large white boxes. They are in a pile, bulging at the sides, and collapsing into each other. My heart lifts and I run to the door. It is like Christmas except I am crying. I place my hand on the boxes. They are warm from sitting in the sun.

Carefully, I bring each box into the house and set it in the corner. I sit down with a cup of coffee and open the first one. Manila file folders are stacked three deep. Each is labeled. There is Dad's novel he wrote when I was a child, his old columns for the *Champaign Courier*, and memoir essays. I read one entitled "Respect." It's a story about a saying my brother and Dad said for years, *up your nose with a rubber hose.* I have long forgotten it, but everything comes rushing back as I read about my younger self insisting I call Dad by his first name, and about my brother, who is so pleased with himself when he tells Dad, *up your nose with a rubber hose.*

In the box are his stories from the memoir classes he's been taking the last two years. Dad had been sending us these stories, but now I reread one with new insight. He's written a story about his life as a child in Japan. He's on his bike and afraid to go through a tunnel. There are a lot of people in the tunnel and he knows he has to go through to get to the other side. He does it, but then realizes he has to return back through the tunnel to get home and to the people he loves. As I reread the essay, written months before his death, I can't help but wonder if he knew something about what might be coming.

I page through the datebooks. My aunt is correct. Dad has kept every card anyone ever sent him. I find Christmas cards I sent, Father's Day cards my sister made, and birthday cards from my brother. As I pick up the last 2009 datebook, a birthday card falls out. I know from my own datebooks that 2009 is the last year Grandpa sent us the books. I open the birthday card. It is from my grandpa, who writes about my grandmother living in a nursing home, and how he still loves her. By 2009, my parents had been divorced for over twenty-five years, yet, my grandpa, my mother's father, still sent birthday cards to Dad as well as the datebooks.

When I reach the final box, I have tears streaming down my face. I have long since stopped drinking my coffee, and it sits cold by my side. I pull out a stack of manila folders filled with recipes. Handwritten recipes, recipes from magazines, and recipes Dad once typed on recipe-file half-sheets of paper. These are the recipes from my childhood, and I thumb through them eagerly. A thick file is filled with Thanksgiving Day recipes, and I pull out *Dad's Turkey*. It's the same recipe he once cooked for us when we were all a family. The following Thanksgiving, my sister and I will cook the turkey using Dad's recipe, and that part of me that always misses Dad will settle down again.

A well-loved and dog-eared recipe sticks out of a folder, and I pull it out. It's one I know well. *Dad's Chex Mix.* It's an old Ralston Purina Recipe from the back of the Chex Mix boxes when dad worked for the company, a recipe which has been changed by Purina and is no longer used. Dad sent Chex Mix to everyone at Christmas. He posted pictures on his Facebook page of the Chex Mix production line where his counter was filled with the snack. Dad boxed up a serving for each person on his list, and tucked it inside Christmas cookie tins. It usually arrived on my doorstep on December 23 or December 24.

This first Christmas without Dad, I make Dad's Chex Mix and box it into four tins—one for my sister, brother, aunt and me. When I take it to be mailed, I am shocked at how much it costs to mail one tiny box of Chex Mix, and realize Dad did this every year on his small Social Security check. By Christmas, my brother and I are no longer speaking due to a disagreement regarding Dad's ashes, something which the grief counselor assured me can be common in families with high emotions over a parent's death, but I send some to him anyway. My brother's Chex Mix package comes back to me on Valentine's Day. My sister says my brother has been traveling, and didn't leave a forwarding address.

My sister, aunt, and I distribute Dad's ashes on a warm and clear evening in mid-September. We go to dinner at a restaurant overlooking Puget Sound and place Dad's box of ashes in the window beside us to watch the passing ferries. My aunt orders his drink of Scotch and water on ice. When the waitress brings it, we set it at the empty place setting. All three of us agree that there is not enough ice in Dad's glass. After dinner, the three of us walk across a parking lot and over a rocky beach to the water's edge. We open Dad's box of ashes and each of us take a handful. The ashes are light in my hand and some sift out to the rocks below. We take turns each saying something about Dad and then letting the ashes go. When it's my turn, I can't speak. My throat clogs with tears and I am, once again, that twelve-year-old girl saying goodbye to Dad in his basement apartment. I toss the ashes into the air and expect them to sink like fireplace ashes, but instead they float away on the light night wind and dance in the air. As we turn from the beach, I feel it. The empty ache inside. It's here. This ache I know so well. I breathe into it like I've been told to do in yoga for a muscle that needs to be stretched. In a minute, it will pass, and by the time we are in the car, the ache is gone and so are Dad's ashes.

When I arrive home, I walk to the box of Dad's writing, stacked in the corner of my dining room, beneath a shrine of Dad's pictures. I place my hand on the boxes beside me filled with all of Dad's manila folders inside, the same type of manila folders I use to keep the kids' poetry before it is published in our books, as well as my own manuscripts as they move through various drafting stages to publication. And like the poetry chapbooks, the poems on the blog, the parents who craved it, the judges and the lawyers who heard it, and the kids who wrote it, I too hear the voice of someone I love.

DAD'S CHEX MIX

½ stick butter
1 ¼ tsp seasoned salt
4 ½ tsp Worcestershire Sauce
2 cups of Chex (corn, rice, wheat)
1 cup salted mixed nuts
1 cup pretzel sticks—break into half

Melt margarine in open roasting pan in preheated 250-degree oven. Stir in seasonings.

Gradually add nuts, pretzels, and cereals; stir to coat evenly.

Bake one hour, stir every 15 minutes. Spread on paper towel to cool. Store in airtight container.

Makes a double batch.

Chuck Hardwick

SIDEWALK TALK

"Hey!" A young man calls to me from across the street of the small, brick post office. I shift my stack of mail from one hand to the other, trying to shield my eyes from the glaring sun so I can see him. Do I know this kid? He's grinning at me, like I should know him, and my mind races. Is he a kid from Jennifer's creative writing class? He's too young to be someone I once taught as a seventh grader. By now, all of my former middle school students are in the last years of college, and a few have families of their own. I see them in the grocery store with a small child in their grocery carts. They stop me and say, "Do you remember me?" Sometimes I do and sometimes I still see that seventh-grade face, but most of the time I don't recognize them any more than I do this boy.

The boy shakes the edges of his baggy orange pants, pants I haven't noticed until now, and he smiles broadly.

There are very few cars on our small main street, and it's easy to walk over to him. "Orange!" He removes his cap and rubs his hand over his short hair.

"Devon!" I say.

With his right hand, Devon continues to shake his baggy pant leg harder. In his left hand, he holds an unlit cigarette and lighter which he moves uncertainly, not sure if I'm going to make an issue of it.

I ignore the cigarette and lighter—after all, I once smoked in high school too.

"You're wearing orange and you're not in there?" I tease him.

Devon turns around, lifts up his shirt, and shows me the stamped letter logo on the back pant. The logo identifies them as belonging to the justice center, not him. Devon nods toward his friend, standing beside him. "You don't know him," he says in a rush. "He doesn't get in trouble."

The other boy's eyes are large and round as he stares at me. I grin at him. I didn't get in trouble either.

"Did you steal these pants?" I ask. I'm trying hard not to start laughing.

Devon shrugs at me and grins. "You live around here?"

"Sorta," I say, suddenly aware that I don't really want him to know where I live—not after the stories he's told us flash through my mind, stories of busting stolen cars through garages and painting graffiti.

Devon nods to confirm my answer will work for him. He continues to hold and twirl his fists in the fabric of his orange pants. "Did the new book come out?" Devon blurts, in the way the kids in detention so often change the subject, swinging their moods from humor to seriousness in an instant.

"The poetry book is published," I say. "Just last week!" Quickly, the memories of Devon flood back, and he becomes much more than just one more boy in orange. Devon is the boy who eagerly wanted to read all the poetry books I brought each week. He can memorize any poem, and the last time he showed off his skill by mouthing along with me as I read the poems in the books, reciting them by heart.

Devon is a boy who loves poetry.

"Is it at the library?" Devon gestures with his thumb to the grey one-story building behind us. It's a tiny library for our town which has grown by leaps and bounds in the last ten years, and I long for a spacious library filled with light and books and old architecture like the one in the next town where I spend afternoons writing.

"I can ask them to have some of the books there." There is a rack filled with pamphlets near the door, and I'm sure the library will be happy to display a few of our books. But I'm not sure they will reach the kids. "Do you see a probation officer? I can leave some at the probation office desk in Denney."

A dark shadow crosses Devon's face. "Yeah. But I think the library would be better."

Quickly, I realize my mistake. Devon wants the poetry books in the community where he lives. He doesn't want them with his parole officer. The poems have no names on them, per the requirements of the detention center, but it doesn't matter to Devon, he wants to be able to walk by the library and say, "A poem I wrote is in that book. In the library." I know the feeling well, and I've been pulling up the e-book listing for *Stained Glass Summer* every time I go into the library.

"The library it is!" I say.

Devon holds out his small child's hand. "Good to see you."

"Out here!" I say, as I take his hand and squeeze firmly, hoping he will stay out here but knowing most likely I will see him again in the poetry workshop at the detention center.

I return to my car, and toss my mail onto the passenger seat. As I pull out of the parking lot, I drive past Devon and his friend. Devon looks up, gives me the high-five signal. His fists grab his pants and he grins and shakes them at me. I give him the thumbs-up signal.

I, too, wear the orange pants.

ACKNOWLEDGEMENTS

This story never could have been written without the brave teen writers whom I met with each week at the Denney Juvenile Justice Center from March 2005–May 2013. Thank you for sharing your stories so honestly with me and giving me the courage to share mine. I have written the moments, events, people and places as I remember them. Minor changes, particularly names and identifying details have been changed to protect the privacy of those in this story. The poems included in this story were originally published in our poetry anthologies with release forms obtained.

Thank you to those who awarded the Denney Poetry Workshop grants, including: The Tulalip Tribes, The Boeing Employees Credit Union Community Grant, The Everett School District Foundation, and The Blanche Miller Trust.

Blanche Miller was a former Snohomish County Juvenile Court Administrator and first woman in the state to be a chief probation officer for a juvenile court. Miller designated a portion of her estate to be used for funding programs that serve court involved youth. The Blanche Miller Trust fund awarded the workshop four grants in order to publish four different collections of the teen's poetry, including: *Please Brave Me, Dry These Tears, Call It Courage, I Am From,* and *Because I Wanted to Be Loved.* These poetry chapbooks were given to the teens at Denney, judges, lawyers, educators, and counselors in the community. (A full listing of the books used in the poetry workshop can be seen at the Behind the Bars Poetry Blog, www.denneypoetry.org)

Gary Marks, School Program Director at Denney Juvenile Justice

Center, opened the door to my first teaching job and later held open the door again to the school day at Denney, giving me his wise council every time we walked down the hall to the units. Margie Holloway took the risk and allowed an unknown writer to work with the kids once a week, and with her staff tirelessly tracked down the release forms for each and every poem included in our chapbooks and blog. Henri Wilson, artist extraordinaire at Denney, guided many of my steps. Ann Teplick mentored me through this path of working with kids in detention and always inspired me to do the work. Richard Gold's beautiful program freed not only the teens' voices, but also my own.

Rev. Mary Omwake's powerful, healing presence comforted me through the death of my dad, and Matthew Wilson's and Richard Held's music lifted my spirit and refreshed my soul during the time surrounding my dad's illness and death.

For those who gave me wise advice in the traveling of this journey in learning to tell my story: Scott Russell Sanders told my young twenty-year-old self, "Go out and live your life before you try and write your memoir;" Kurt Caswell took this story in its many parts and patiently tried to make sense of it; Pamela Greenwood read the manuscript and kindly asked me to dig one layer deeper into my story; and Rhay Christou talked me off the ledge more times than I can count and convinced me with her belief that I could write this story—thank you.

Thank you to the team who helped produce the book including: Sarah Cloots who worked as copy editor, Su Kopil at Earthly Charms who designed the cover art and Kelly Shorten at KMD Web Designs who did the book's layout and formats. Thank you.

Thank you to my grandparents, whose final gift of generosity gave me what every writer needs a "room of my own" and to my siblings, aunt and mom, who allowed me to tell this story. Any errors in the telling or the perception are mine.

And, finally, thank you to my dad, who at my college graduation gave me Tobias Wolfe's *This Boy's Life* and said to me, "We all come from somewhere, and we all have places to go in life. We don't have much control over the former, but we can control the direction of the latter. Think about it as you go forward in your life's journey." From one writer to another, thank you, Dad.

A portion of the proceeds from *Kids in Orange* will be donated to the Denney Juvenile Justice Center as a grant to be used to hire writers to work with teens at Denney.

END

BOOKS BY MINDY

Stained Glass Summer

Weaving Magic

Seymour's Secret

Sweetheart Cottage

Sweetheart Summer

STAINED GLASS SUMMER

Enjoy an excerpt from Stained Glass Summer

CHAPTER ONE

"Art Power," Dad says.

I move my finger over the amethyst oval stone set inside a silver ring that looks very expensive. I've gotten used to Dad's outrageous, impractical art presents, like the tall, pink glass vase he gave me last Christmas. It's part of being an artist's daughter, and I love it.

"Fabulous!" I've been waiting to use that word on something after I heard an art judge at one of Dad's shows exclaim, "Fabulous!" when she handed him the first place ribbon. I wave my hand over Dad's photography books on the coffee table and admire the carved leaves and swirls that don't completely cover my tanned ring finger.

"It's too expensive for a twelve-year-old," Mom says as she enters the room. She carries a white cake with twelve candles. Her dark hair bounces with every step. It's the same color as mine, only hers is curly and mine is straight. My eyes meet Mom's, and I look away. I know she's right. Dad's gifts are too expensive. But I love Dad's fabulous art gifts, and I'm not going to give them up.

"Wish for a win in that contest," Dad says as Mom sets the cake on the coffee table. His eyes sparkle as he leans forward. I notice the small bit of gray in his hair that frames his narrow face

I know not to say anything. Dad doesn't believe in getting old. I think about the school art contest. The winner gets to take summer classes at the Chicago Art Institute, where Dad teaches. I'm already imagining what will happen when I win. I'll spend the whole summer with Dad. We'll ride together to the Institute, and I'll take my classes while he teaches his.

Afterward, we'll ride home together and talk about our day. But even more importantly, I must win to prove that I'm an award-winning artist like Dad.

My stomach cramps as I think about trying to prove that I am an award-winning artist. I take a deep breath, and lean over to blow the candles. All of the candles blow out, but one remains. Its flickering flame is like a taunting tease.

"Oh no," I moan. "It's bad luck!"

Dad exhales, and in one whoosh he blows the last candle out. He turns to me, and his eyes are cold and unreadable. "I trust you to take good care of the ring. The Andes artist says it has power."

"Seeing the future?" I run my hand over the purple stone. The stone warms under my touch, as if powers are seeping from the ring's stone into my hand and back again. I'd love to see the future. I rub my finger over the smooth stone and wait for Dad to tell me about the ring. I love Dad's travel stories. He entertains Mom and me with world adventures in different languages, new customs, and exotic foods.

"Power," Dad says. "Power for your art."

"Mmm..." I say, hoping I sound very serious. I know about art power. There can be nothing on the canvas, yet there are a million things waiting to be born. Art transfers me out of one time and into another. I love to look at the clock and, when I check again, five hours have passed. Some days the ideas come rushing forward while other days nothing comes at all. But I always like the surprise of never knowing when the ideas might pop up.Mom clears her throat, and I look up to see her holding a piece of cake on a sunflower paper plate and a Happy Birthday napkin. As I take the plate, our fingers touch, and I grin. Mom stopped at the bakery down the street to pick out the most expensive cake in the store. Mom likes expensive presents just as much as Dad does.

I lift my fork to take a bite and watch as Mom tries to hand Dad a piece of cake. He frowns and shakes his head at her. For a minute, a hurt look darkens Mom's face. It's the same one I feel when he has something else to do and I'm annoying him. Something that happens a lot and I try not to think about.

Dad doesn't notice Mom's look. He never does. In Dad's world, there is one person— Dad. Mom and I say that is what makes him such a good photographer. But sometimes I wish that he weren't such a good photographer, and a better dad instead.

Dad stretches. His six-foot frame reaches toward the high ceilings, and I swear that if he stands on tiptoes, he can reach the ceiling beams with his long, tapered fingers. "I'm headed upstairs."

"Can I come with you?" I ask softly, and stare at the floor. I can't look at Dad. There's too much hope inside me. Hope that too often goes unfulfilled.

"Just for a little bit. I want you to finish up that collage for the contest. I'll make sure everything looks perfect."

"Everything looks great!" I pop off the couch and leave my untouched piece of cake on the coffee table next to Dad's photography books.

"Jasmine." Mom touches my arm briefly, and I want to shake her away. I know what she's trying to tell me. Don't get too excited. You know how he is. This moment isn't really about you; it never is. It's about Dad. But I don't want to hear her, not now. Not on my birthday. Instead, I want to believe that this moment is about me. I want to believe that this time will be different.

"The contest," I say, while hoping Mom understands my unspoken words. It's okay this time. "Dad has to help me finish my collage."

Mom shakes her head and turns away from me. She reaches to the coffee table beside her. "I have something for you too." Mom turns around, holding a thick catalogue between her fingers. "I wanted to surprise you." She pauses and then says, "I bought you special summer school lessons."

"Art classes?" Mom bought me art classes! I am so excited I can barely breathe. My birthday is turning out to be fabulous.

"Not exactly." Mom shakes her head, and her dark brown hair moves from side to side across her shoulders. "These classes are at the private high school. It's the school where I attended." There is a bit of hesitancy in her voice, as if she's worried I won't remember all the times she has told me about her high school. "I thought you'd like to get a head start for when you're ready for high school. If you start now in summer classes with a foreign language, then in a few years you'll be very prepared for the high school classes."

"Oh," I say, trying not to hurt Mom, but it doesn't take much to hear the deflation in my voice, as if I am a balloon that has just lost all its air. I twist my fingers together. I do appreciate her gift. But I am an artist. I need summer art classes with Dad, not classes at Fishers.

"Fishers is a good school," Mom says quietly.

"Please, Mom," I beg. The words tumble out before I can stop them. It's a conversation Mom and I have had a zillion times. No one ever wins.

Mom slowly sets down the catalogue. She lifts her plate and takes a bite of her cake. Her red painted lips close over her fork as the cake slides into her mouth. I've disappointed her, and I feel bad. Most of the time, Mom and I are a team. We have to be. It takes two of us to live with Dad, and even then, I'm not sure we ever really win.

I try to explain to Mom. "You'll see. I'm going to win the contest. It will all be okay." I reach out and give Mom a small pat, as if she is the child and I'm the adult. "I promise. It will all work out."

Mom smiles sadly at me. "Okay, Jasmine," she says.

I twirl around and head toward the loft spiral stairs. I know that, this time, things will work out.

As I climb the spiral staircase into the studio loft, I hear Dad walking above me. I can't help but hum. I love nighttime in Dad's studio. It's taken me a long time to earn Dad's trust. On my first visit to the studio, I tried to color on one of Dad's paintings. I thought the white box outline in the middle of the white canvas needed some color. Dad caught me as I was busy scribbling away. He grabbed my hand, and the crayon dropped to the floor. He didn't say anything for what seemed like forever. And then, with his voice of steel, said, "If you're going to do art, I will teach you."

Now, I watch as Dad pours hot water from a small silver pot that rests on a warming plate in the far right corner of the loft. "Hot chocolate?"

"Yes." I head for the rack of mugs perched on a shelf below a window overlooking Lake Michigan. There are mugs with scenes of Australian beaches and oceans, and other mugs with African lions, giraffes, and elephants. I pick up one of these mugs and hope the power of the animal will jump off the cup and I'll roar.

I pour hot water from the pot and eye the row of Dad's pictures hanging on the white wall. A small light highlights each. I know each photo by heart. Each framed picture has a blue or silver award tacked to the frame: Best New Photographer for the State of Illinois, First Place in the Mid-West Photography Winter Exhibit, First Place in the Chicago Photography and Design Show. The rows stretch twelve across. This spring, Dad has started hanging a second row under the first.

"Yours will be right next to mine," Dad says when he sees me looking at the pictures. He points to a blank space. There is a hook already attached to the wall.

I bite the inside of my cheek and taste a small amount of blood. I have to win the contest. If I want to be an artist like Dad, I have to start my own wall of awards. And, even more importantly, I have to prove that he has the best daughter in the world, and the only way to do that is by winning art contests.

I turn around and look at my contest entry, which is laid out on a long easel. Dad has been helping me and adding touches while I haven't been in the studio, but something doesn't seem right. He's added a bit of texture for a three-dimensional appearance. But I'm not quite sure that the colors blend in the far right hand corner. I want to say something to Dad, but I know what he'll say. "In order to compete, you must stand out. Yours must be different than everyone else's."

I rub my fingers over my new ring's purple stone and hear a whisper. I'm not sure if it's my imagination, but I think I hear the stone say, "You will win the contest." Dad said it had magic powers.

"Are you going to get started?" Dad asks. He perches on a metal stool with a brown cushion in front of his computer. He waves his hand toward the canvas.

"Just thinking." I smile at Dad. "Preparing." Dad always says that half of art is preparing — thinking about what you want to accomplish before you sit down and start to draw.

"Well, don't prepare all night." Dad checks his watch. "I need to sleep."

I'm suddenly nervous again. I know the rules. In the art studio, we follow Dad's rules.

I dip a large paintbrush into green paint and wipe the edges against a water jar. For a minute, doubts crowd my mind as I study my painting. Dad chose an extra-large canvas from the art shop. I'm not sure how I'll get the canvas to school without a ride, and getting a dependable ride from Dad is not always easy.

"I just got busy," he'll say as I open the car door, after forty minutes of waiting outside the Art Palace Community Hall on Saturday mornings. It's always embarrassing, waiting for Dad. The last Art Palace teacher to leave always asks if I'm sure that I didn't need a ride home. And they always give me that look. It's the one that is half-pity and half-worry, while I try to make up excuses for where Dad is and why he forgets his daughter.

I once tried to be mad at Dad about his lateness, but as soon as I got in the car, he turned to me and said, "Don't give me attitude or I won't pick you up at all." The last thing I want is for Dad not to pick me up at all.

I love my time with Dad — even if he is a little late. I study my painting and say softly, "Dad?" "Mmm…"

"You're taking me to the school contest tomorrow, right?" Dad stops and raises his eyebrows.

I know this look and it frightens me.

"Why are you asking?" Dad snaps. "I told you I'd take you. Don't ask again."

"Right," I say as my stomach churns. I don't know why I asked. I knew Dad would take me. Sometimes I just do stupid things. This time, I have broken Art Studio Rule Number 2: No disturbing the artist at work.

I shift on my stool and turn my attention back to the painting. There is something about the colors that doesn't sit right with me. In my mind, I picture them alive and vibrant. But on the page they seem dull and flat. I stare out the window and into the tall dark trees surrounding the studio. If only I could capture the green, or even the amber, orange and yellow when the oak tree leaves turn in the fall.

And then, as if a genie has hopped off the tree and said, "Your wish is my command," light green, dark green and leafy textures swirl around me. It is as if I have left my body and I am flying in the trees. It reminds me of when Dad takes me to the amusement park and I ride the roller coasters. When my heart beats a million miles an hour, as the small carts careen close to the edges and around loops but always, held by a small chain, holding me above the hard ground.

In my art trance, I am flying up and down the tree limbs. I reach toward the sky and then, sensing that I can't crash into the ground, dive back toward the roots of the tree. Everything buzzes, hums, and vibrates around me in a symphony of sound as I dance on one limb and then the other. I am flying in tune to my own harmonized orchestra.

The studio casts light into the tree and I fly over to the window. Dad shifts and moves images on his computer. My mind whirls. Am I really in the tree? How has it happened? I feel so free. It's as if possibilities are all around me and nothing can stop me. Every artist must know this feeling! The green fades, and my hands grasp my paintbrush. The paint smell of the studio engulfs me.

"Dad!"

"Yes?" Dad doesn't take his eyes off the computer screen.

I stop. What will Dad think when I tell him about this world?

But I can't keep it in. I have to tell him.

"Yes?" Dad repeats and peers at me over his thin-wire rimmed glasses.

"I danced in the tree limbs. Everything was so green! Can you do that?" I hop off my stool.

"Maybe it's the muse," Dad says. "Or maybe it's part of that magic ring. You know I always choose great gifts for you."

"Yes," I say. "You always choose great gifts." I twirl my ring as I think about where I have just been. The world is my own private art world. I can go there anytime I need ideas or inspiration. It's a bit like magic, and now I must give the world a name. When I was younger, I lined up all the stuffed animals on my bed and gave them each a name. Not just a first name, but a last name too. I chose names that sounded exotic to me, names like Hamish and Rhianna.

The name for my magical art world has to be something special. Something unique. Something like...Lucianna. The name pops into my head and I remember Lucy Ann, my best friend in elementary school, who arrived in second grade with a new pink pencil case, sharpened colored pencils and fresh watercolor paints. She was my best friend until she moved at the end of fourth grade, and I haven't had another friend like her.

"Jasmine," Dad says, his voice suddenly sharp. "Get back to work. I've got some other things to do."

I nod as the familiar feeling of not wanting to bother Dad washes over me. I don't want to annoy Dad. I'm not always important to him, but I want to be.

I drop a splotch of green onto my canvas. The paint spreads out, leaving thin spider legs behind like cracks in a sheet of glass. I can't help but think that I am like a sheet of glass, cracking under the pressure of Dad.

CHAPTER TWO

Mom parks the Toyota in front of Lakeview Middle School. The morning sun has already moved across the tops of the gymnasium, and I know I'm very late.

I waited too long for Dad.

At breakfast, he said that he just had to run out for a little bit. The morning light was perfect. But as the stove clock ticked past the first bell, I knew Dad had forgotten his promise. He had forgotten this was the morning he had to take me to school for the contest. I try very hard not to start bawling. There is some simple explanation, I keep telling myself. There must be. He told me he would take me.

"Jasmine," Mom says.

I look at her, and our eyes lock.

"I'm okay," I mumble. Once again, Mom and I are a team. As our eyes meet, I feel tears floating too close to the surface. I swallow hard and push them away. I turn around and try to lift the collage out of the backseat. The sides jam against the seats. I hold my breath and hope that the canvas won't tear. If Dad were here, he'd park the car and very carefully ease the collage out of it. But Dad isn't here.

I push and tug, and the collage breaks free. I hold it in front of me like a shield and head toward the gymnasium. I hate being late for anything, so I walk quickly.

"Art projects over here!" Mrs. Hanson, the school principal, calls as I step through the gymnasium doors. Her nasal voice carries across the slick floor and bounces off the concrete walls. "Jasmine! You're late," she barks.

"I'm sorry." I peek around my collage and spy an empty easel near the front. Dad always says, "Get there early and set up in the front. By the time the judges get to the back, everything looks the same to them. They'll remember the first one they see." The wave of disappointment that Dad is not here to help washes over me. My throat closes and I push away Dad's face, sending the sad feelings deeper and deeper into a dark hole inside of me that I imagine burying with a big shovel under a lot of dirt.

I hoist my collage onto the easel. The easel tilts and sways under the weight of the heavy canvas. I keep my hand on the collage and try to find a balancing point.

"That yours?"

"Yes." I don't need to turn around to know the voice.

"Kinda strange. Don't you think?" Julie Ann, my worst enemy, steps so close to me I can smell her peach-scented lotion. She scrunches her nose and crosses her arms. I want to do the same about the lotion she is wearing. Julie Ann sticks her face close to the collage.

"It's art," I say as the easel tilts to the right. I lurch after it in a stretch that was never taught in gym class. I will not fight with Julie Ann. Last year, after arguing with her about space on an art table, I spent three days in the counseling office, sitting in a green plastic chair with a rip in the side, while Mr. McIntosh talked about the importance of conflict resolution. I pretended to be interested.

"Hmm…" Julie Ann places her pink-painted fingernail alongside the collage and moves it slowly. At any minute her long nail will tear a gaping hole in the canvas.

"Don't!" I knock Julie Ann's finger away and bite the inside of my lip as the canvas tips and the easel crashes to the floor.

My collage lands facedown on the hard gymnasium floor. "Jasmine!" Mrs. Hansen bustles toward us and leaves two parents standing, mouths open and pencils poised above clipboards.

"See you later." Julie Ann smirks and ducks around the corner of a watercolor print with sunflowers.

Wanting to slug Julie Ann, I pick up my collage. If Dad were here, Julie Ann never would have dreamed of talking to me. I push down the lump in my throat and ball my fingers into a tight clutch around my collage. For a minute, I want to scream. How can the morning light be more important than me? How can he have forgotten about the art contest? And just as quickly, I stuff the words deep inside.

It's something I learned to do a long time ago.

"Set your collage over there," Mrs. Hansen says and waves to a back corner of the gymnasium. She pushes red curls away from her fore- head. The curls spring and then bound back onto her shiny forehead.

"What about the judges?" The parent judges cluster in the corner. They are all staring at us, and I want to stick out my tongue. But I know that would really disqualify me.

"They'll find it," Mrs. Hansen mutters and walks away.

A spot way in the back is not a good idea, but the alternative of arguing with Mrs. Hansen seems worse. I pick up the collage and carry it to the back corner. Once I reach the corner, I see there is no easel. Only a small doorway leading to what I assume must be the janitor's closet. I lean the collage against the closed door and step back to take one last look. I hope it doesn't slip and crash to the floor.

In the shadows, the colors blend together into one dark mass. The brilliant green from the tree and my vision of the night before is non-existent. My insides feel just like those colors— blended in one dark mass, tucked away in the corner.

The morning drags, and I can barely concentrate. I'm thinking of nothing but the contest. After a lunch that I don't eat, I join a slow-moving line of people heading toward the auditorium and the contest awards. The chatter rises and falls in a big bunch of noise around me. Seeing the line snake toward the back of the auditorium, I jump out and head toward the front. I can't sit in the back. I need to be up front. Winners sit up front. Up front is closer to where I will jump up on the stage and claim my award.

"Jasmine!" Mr. McIntosh steps forward and places his large hand on my shoulder. "Your class is in row 12." He gently turns me toward the middle of the auditorium.

"I'm in the contest," I remind him. "I sit in the front." I give him my best smile. I hope he will not say anything about my rebellious behavior with Julie Ann.

He mumbles something about forgetting, and I dodge around him, plop into a front row seat and take a deep breath. Just because I have been in his office for that one fight with Julie Ann, it seems like I can't do anything without having him right behind me and checking every move. I cross my legs and twirl my ring. In only a matter of minutes, my name will be called and I'll be up on that stage. I will prove to Mr. McIntosh and everyone else that I am not a failure.

Jasmine Baast, Artist. I hum as I imagine hanging my collage next to Dad's award winning photography.

On stage, Mrs. Hansen begins talking. The seats around me remain empty. I try not to think about how I am sitting in the front.

Alone.

Everyone else sits with friends.

For a minute, I pretend I have a very important phone call and dig in my bag for my cell phone. Maybe Dad will have remembered to text me a message. A good luck message. I will smile and not feel so alone. I flip open the top and stare hard at the screen.

There is no message.

"And now," Mrs. Hansen says, "The contest winners."

I twirl my ring hard and fast. My heart feels like it might pound right out of my chest.

"Third place..." Mrs. Hansen says. "Goes to..." I hold my breath.

"Vicky Parkinson for her watercolor drawing, Flowers in the Garden."

A tiny girl with long dark hair sprints toward the podium from the left side of the auditorium, and a group of girls scream. Vicky Parkinson is a sixth grader. I clap and smile one of Mom's "everything is just wonderful" smiles. She uses those smiles a lot after Dad has said something that is not so wonderful.

"Second place," Mrs. Hansen says, and turns toward the seventh grade bleachers. "Alex Cooper for his Day at the Baseball Park photograph."

A blonde boy, who I think might be cute in a few years, jogs forward to the podium. I clap while smiling at him. Scooting to the edge of the chair, I hold my breath.

"And now," Mrs. Hansen says as Alex steps to the side of the stage next to Vicky. "The moment you've been waiting for. The first place winner."

I let out a big whoosh of air.

"We've had many fine entries, and the judges had a hard time deciding."

Why do they always say that? I shift closer to the edge of my chair.

"The winner..." Mrs. Hansen pauses. "Is Julie Ann Wilson."

I freeze. Julie Ann.

Julie Ann with her flimsy watercolor. Sunflowers in a meadow.

That's not art. Art is my collage.

Bold. Big.

And fabulous.

I jump up and instead of cheering, I scream. "Didn't you see the collage in the corner?"

No one pays attention to me as Julie Ann steps on to the stage. She takes her award and ribbon from Mrs. Hansen and turns to give a victory wave.

I push out of my seat and rush toward the front podium. I don't care if I get in trouble and have to spend days and days in the ripped chair in the counseling office.

Julie Ann smirks. "Are you here to congratulate me?" She waves her blue ribbon and white envelope in front of her. "Or give me suggestions for what to buy with my gift certificate?"

I shove past Julie Ann and toward Mrs. Hanson. "My collage. Did you judge my collage?"

Mrs. Hanson frowns at me. "Only winners on the stage."

"My collage! No one saw my collage!" I can barely keep the tears from spilling over as I cross my hands across my chest and try to stop myself from shaking. Why is this happening? I should be the winner.

"No." Mrs. Hanson shakes her head. "You are disqualified. Your canvas is too big."

I hold very still, like I do when Mom and Dad fight. I lie in the dark as I listen to their voices rise, thinking that, somehow, I can make the fighting stop with my stillness.

I remember showing the contest directions to Dad, the ones that said the size of canvas we could enter. Dad pushed the paper aside and said, "The size of your canvas is not going to matter, Jasmine. They don't really care about things like that."

"No." I barely whisper the word. No. The shaking feeling is back, only it's much worse than it was last night. I have failed. Mom will make me attend summer classes at Fishers. Dad will go to his art institute classes without me, and I will be nothing.

Nothing.

I shove my way off the stage and head toward the exit doors. Who cares if it's the emergency exit and the alarm will ring? This is an emergency, and there has to be something I can do to stop the train wreck that is about to become my summer.

I reach out for the exit doors as Mr. McIntosh drops his heavy hand on my right shoulder. "Can I see you in my office please?"

I whirl around in time to see Julie Ann shake her head and smirk. I want to sink into the floor. I have lost the art contest. I've disappointed Dad, and I'm going to spend days in after-school detention. Everything is more than a train wreck. It is a tsunami.

BUY STAINED GLASS SUMMER TO CONTINUE READING

ABOUT MINDY HARDWICK

Mindy Hardwick holds an MFA in Writing for Children and Young Adults from Vermont College. Her published books for children and young adults include: *Stained Glass Summer, Weaving Magic,* and *Finders Keepers.* She also writes sweet contemporary romance including her Cranberry Bay Series: *Sweetheart Cottage* and *Sweetheart Summer.* Mindy is included on the Washington State Teaching Artist Roster and frequently teaches workshops to young writers. She facilitated a poetry workshop for teens at Denney Juvenile Justice Center and has written a memoir about that experience. Mindy can often be found walking with her cocker spaniel, Stormy, on the north Oregon Coast beaches and dreaming up new story ideas. Visit her website: www.mindyhardwick.com.

22167435R00117

Made in the USA
San Bernardino, CA
09 January 2019